CONTENTS

*

ILLUSTRATIONS

*

ACKNOWLEDGMENT

All of the illustrations are reproduced by courtesy of the Schiller-Nationalmuseum in Marbach am Neckar.

TRANSLATOR'S PREFACE

*

The publications which, in 1959, marked the bicentenary of Schiller's birth revealed a much profounder concern with the status of a great national figure than can usually be detected in the pious tributes such occasions provoke. What emerged clearly from these studies was the conviction of many of the most distinguished scholars of the day that Schiller is and will always remain a seminal influence in German intellectual life, despite the characteristic fluctuations in his popular appeal. It is true that the image of Schiller the impassioned humanitarian idealist has little to offer an age grown weary of words and urgent calls to self-transcendence; and yet it is equally true that without Schiller German letters, poetry, historical and aesthetic thought and, above all, the living theatre in the German-speaking countries would be disastrously impoverished. It is for this reason that modern scholarship is concerned to rediscover the essential Schiller and to reassess the relevance for the modern world of works which have become all too familiar, and difficult to focus on that account.

The results of the new approach reveal just how superficial was the old view of Schiller as the idol of a nation's youth: indeed, so dark are the insights he is now shown to have had into the ambiguity of the human dilemma, into the loneliness (*Don Carlos*) and enforced deceit (*Maria Stuart*) inseparable from autocratic rule, into the metaphysical malaise that can be precipitated when action is at war with reflection (*Wallenstein*) and with doubts as to ultimate identity (*Demetrius*), that the change in attitude cannot be regretted. The moral idealism – legacy of an age which believed it possible for men to pull themselves out of the mire by their own bootstraps – no longer appeals: we now realize that it was but one aspect of Schiller, frequently masking the iron realism of his profounder poetic intuitions. As long ago as 1905 Hugo von Hofmannsthal predicted that Schiller would ultimately be thought of, not as Germany's great advocate, pleading the cause of freedom before the thrones of kings, but as her conquistador, a great adventurer of the spirit, annexing the intellectual worlds of Kantian philosophy, of the Ancients, of Catholicism, and ruling in them as did Napoleon in every capital of Europe, an imperious stranger. In his art as in his life (since, in this case, the two are inseparable), it is the boldness of the gesture that arrests our attention and compels our assent; and it is this, too, that conditions Bernt von Heiseler's approach to Schiller.

In the foreword to his little collection of lives of the German poets, *Lebenswege der Dichter* (1957), Herr von Heiseler tells us that when he sat down in 1929 to write about his famous father, Henry von Heiseler, the idea came to him of dividing his time between the composition of original plays and of a series of such biographies. His purpose would be to present Germany's greatest poets in a manner which would at one and the same time interpret their works and trace the trajectory of their lives in such a way as to reveal the essential nature of both in its relevance for their nation. He said this of the four studies in *Lebenswege der Dichter*, which were all his other distinguished activities as a poet, novelist and playwright had enabled him to complete up till then; but it is clear that his biography of Schiller, written for the bicentenary year, is cast in the same mould. A poet's life should be told, he said, as a saga is told; it should be a saga, not because of its proneness to mythical accretions, but because a saga reveals the core of its subject's character. A saga presupposes a hero: and it is precisely this heroic quality in Schiller – of whom Goethe said that he was magnificent even when cutting his fingernails – which conforms so well to Heiseler's approach. Moreover, the consistency of his viewpoint, and his desire to grasp and present Schiller in his significance as a German phenomenon, combine to render his study most suitable for introducing the non-German student to Germany's greatest dramatic poet.

The book is consistent in its moral, as well as its formal, attitude. Bernt von Heiseler writes as a convinced Christian, and although unswerving in his admiration for Schiller both as a creative artist and as a man, he does not hesitate to take him to task when his eighteenth-century faith in human perfectibility leads Schiller to view salvation as attainable through autonomous moral effort rather than conformity with supernatural grace. Thus, while emphasizing the enduring worth of Schiller's unique insights into the nature of aesthetic activity in the *Ästhetische Briefe*, he criticizes the way in which the treatise equates moral and aesthetic values; he acknowledges the incidental excellences of *Die Jungfrau von Orleans* (*The Maid of Orleans*), but considers the subject unsuitable for Schiller because the category of the sacred eludes his creative grasp, despite his wry tribute to its existence in *Das Glück* (*Good Fortune*). Such an attitude is both stimulating and legitimate: in making moral (as opposed to purely aesthetic) judgments, a concealed relativism is ultimately no less arbitrary than a fairly-exercised committed approach, and, lacking a cutting edge, probably reveals less.

In translating Herr von Heiseler's book into English it was thought advisable to render the original German, which, in conformity with his avowed method, is that of a practising poet rather than a professional critic, as closely as possible; nevertheless, it was found necessary to take a number of minor liberties with the text, consisting chiefly of small alterations and omissions designed to render a study addressed initially to a German public more generally suitable for English readers. Following the same policy, a critical apparatus has been added consisting of footnotes explaining literary and historical references, a brief bibliography, a chronology of Schiller's life and works, synopses of the plays, and an index. Quotations from literary works are given in the original German with footnote translations; all other quotations are put directly into English.

JOHN BEDNALL

University College of North Wales
Bangor, 1961

AUTHOR'S INTRODUCTION

*

We no longer like using the word 'immortality' to describe that fame which, for a time, is the after-glow of a great man's life; and words denoting length, let alone permanence of duration, have become difficult for us to pronounce. For even the greatest of poets only endures in his language, and a language can die just as the nation that speaks it can die – not only as did the Greeks and Romans, who lived to see their inheritors and be their teachers, but die and leave no heirs behind, like the culture of a lost Atlantis. Would anyone care to maintain, today, that this could not happen to us as well?

Granted the possibility, there are still two attitudes one can adopt. We see many of our contemporaries clinging to the present, which, for them, is no longer a sacred mission linking past and future, but merely a fleeting habitation; and they are unwilling to think beyond it. They would like us to call them vital, living to the top of their bent in the fullness of the moment, but the expression of this attitude is associated with too much strain and over-eagerness for it really to merit the description. The second attitude is based on the conviction that a nation can only overcome the danger which threatens its existence by the essential truth of its claim on life. In just such a way one sees the fir-tree which has been buried by a landslide thrusting its tender yet vigorous tip up through the rubble.

One purpose of this book is to demonstrate that the figure of Schiller, and his works, are one of the vital forces in German life, essential and indispensable both now and in the future. For the nineteenth century this was a foregone conclusion, and will be so again – that is, if Germany survives the present dark day in her history. Today it cannot be denied that Germans' consciousness of themselves is dimmed, and that this dimming has also greatly influenced their attitude to German Classical literature. Classicism was by no means the only, although certainly the last, great form in which the German spirit was manifested; in the Romantic Age it appeared amorphous, a sign of activity, a call, but no more; while what came afterwards never attained to a spiritual form in which it could speak to the world, and for that reason remained odd and enigmatic. The voice of German Classicism was once heard throughout the world; today it is as if it were forgotten; its great figures hardly make any impact among Germany's neighbours, their names do not live through their works. Does anyone still know and read them? And one is more or less forced to admit that the situation is no better in Germany itself; school-readings tend, by and large, to promote misunderstanding rather than to serve as an introduction, since German Classical literature, for all its seemingly transparent clarity, has a greater depth than a young mind can appreciate. And the theatres, as they are run at present, are unable truly to interpret the Classical plays, for they are out of sympathy with that overflowing of the emotions which finds expression in the language of Classicism. This means that partial knowledge is communicated, which may be considered worse than none at all; but it has distorted Schiller's image, and did so earlier and even more seriously than it did that of Goethe.

The following pages represent an attempt, not to controvert other views of Schiller, but to depict the man, his life and his works. It would be good if this could be done with as much freshness as though it were for the very first time.

CHAPTER I

FAMILY AND BACKGROUND

*

The Schillers are a Lutheran family from Swabia. Johann Kaspar, the poet's father, travelled widely in the service of various masters as a field-surgeon, soldier and later as an officer. Wherever he went he kept his eyes open and was quick to learn. As a young man he travelled to the Netherlands and doubtless described to his son the Dutch nation's virtues and love of liberty. Among the many curious experiences he recorded, the following seems particularly characteristic because of the way he describes it: 'At the siege of Bergen in Hainault, whilst in the trenches as a private soldier in von Diesbach's Franco-Swiss regiment, having on account of undue pressure of duty been unable to snatch more than an hour or two of sleep in several days and nights, I was so overcome by weariness that I lay down in a cornfield behind the trench and slept by my reckoning a full twelve hours. When I awoke at about two in the afternoon, I found the whole area round about ploughed up by shell-bursts, whilst I myself was partly buried in sand.' A note in the margin reads: 'N.B. a broad-bean field.'

He returned home to Swabia riding his own horse and with a useful sum of money put by, and married, at the age of twenty-five, Elisabeth Dorothea Kodweiss, the seventeen-year-old only daughter of the landlord of the Lion at Marbach. 'That splendid woman,' says a later description of her, 'was tall, slender and shapely; her hair was fair, almost reddish, whilst her eyes gave evidence of a sickly constitution. Her face was full of gentleness and depth of feeling, her broad forehead betokened the thinking woman.'

Kodweiss handled his money badly and seems also to have had bad luck; the family's circumstances deteriorated, and Kaspar Schiller, unable to stop the rot, took service again as an ensign and adjutant in the army of his sovereign, Karl Eugen of Württemberg, who was obliged, in order to obtain French subsidies, to fight in the Seven Years War against Frederick the Great. Kaspar Schiller went as far as Silesia with the Württemberg corps, and was at the Battle of Leuthen (1757), the point at which the war took a decisive turn in Frederick's favour. On the retreat he wandered into a marsh and nearly drowned. When an epidemic broke out he tended his patients with self-sacrificing devotion. In 1758 when he returned home from the field for the first time with a lieutenant's commission his wife greeted him with a daughter, Christophine. In 1759 he again had to leave home. His wife visited him in camp at Ludwigsburg. While there, she felt her time approaching, returned quickly to Marbach, and on November 10th – which is also Luther's birthday – she bore a son, Johann Christoph Friedrich. The news that a son had been born to him followed the lieutenant, whose regiment was already on the march, and when the message reached him he offered a prayer to the 'Supreme Being'* that his son might receive those powers of mind to which he himself, through lack of education, had been unable to attain. Friedrich remained the only son; four daughters were born after him, two of whom died in infancy. Besides Christophine, therefore, only Luise and Christiane (called Nanette) grew up with him, the latter a late arrival twelve years younger than her brother.

Marbach, the home of his mother's family, had not yet recovered from the last time the French had come to the Central Neckar region, when it had been completely burnt down. It is a very old town situated high above the river in pleasant, fertile surroundings. But Friedrich can only have had very

* German 'Wesen aller Wesen'.

indistinct memories of the neighbourhood, for he was scarcely four years old when the Schillers moved to Schwäbisch-Gmünd, and soon after that to Lorch. Perhaps the busy camp-life of the soldiery which he later depicted in such masterly fashion is a lingering recollection of the times when his mother visited his father in his different garrisons and took Fritz with her. For, since 1761, Kaspar was once more in Württemberg, and his regiment was quartered in Urach, Cannstatt, Ludwigsburg, Stuttgart and then Ludwigsburg again; the lieutenant rose to the rank of captain, and as such became in 1763 a recruiting-officer charged with the recruiting of soldiers for his Duke in the Imperial City of Schwäbisch-Gmünd. The family's removal to the neighbouring hamlet of Lorch took place because it was cheaper to live there.

That Karl Eugen should have been obliged to send recruiting-officers 'abroad' (i.e. to a town which did not belong to Württemberg) is probably due to the fact that, as a result of the second agreement on subsidies which he made with France in 1758, his own dukedom was completely denuded of men capable of bearing arms. These acts of tyranny on which a judgment was passed in *Kabale und Liebe* (*Love and Intrigue*),* which echoes across two centuries, must have been well known to the elder Schiller, yet, in the notes he made for his autobiography, this man who was so conscientious in other directions made not a single mention of them; on the contrary, when he came to speak about the uprisings in the land, he attributed them to false rumours spread by disaffected persons. It is amazing to see the matter-of-fact way in which his loyalty as an officer guides his pen at this point, and to recognize how stern was the sense of a subject's duties which prevailed in the Schiller household, a loyalty to the ruler which did not permit criticism even of insupportable wrongs. Karoline von Wolzogen, Schiller's sister-in-law, speaks of the simple moral tone which reigned in the household. 'Honour and tender consideration for the women in the family circle were the keynotes of the

* Schiller's third play (1783).

atmosphere in which the boy [Schiller] grew up. The father had that good breeding which comes from the heart.' Although the woman who wrote this description was the child of an age which observed and sought to emphasize the noble rather than the uncouth, nevertheless we can see that it was not an environment calculated to breed a revolutionary; if Friedrich Schiller became a revolutionary, it was his Duke who made him one.

In order to complete the picture of Schiller's father, his passion for economic reform should be mentioned. He made a collection of his own and other people's observations and opinions, he published a book *Beiträge zur Beförderung des bürgerlichen Wohlstandes* (*Contributions to the Advancement of Civil Wellbeing*); his thought and his writings were directed towards practical activity. He had a great love of trees, and when he was finally transferred from Lorch to Ludwigsburg he planted a tree-nursery behind his house. The Duke learned of this and had him brought to The Solitude.* Under Kaspar Schiller's care tens of thousands of trees grew from the stony soil, trees which he supplied for roads and parks; he was the founder of an economical system of fruit-tree growing, and his nursery became a sight which people travelled from all parts of the world to see. He was so wrapped up in these interests that he was quite capable of forgetting his nearest and dearest on their account: even the gentle Elisabeth Dorothea permits herself, in an intimate letter to her son in 1796, the despairing outburst: 'A maid could just as well attend to his needs as a wife. To his own folk he has for many years behaved with complete indifference, and he is ever more concerned with pandering to his own whims and fancies and carrying out whatever notion may come into his head, than with their well-being.' We also hear tell of his hardness towards the peasants who had to do carting for The Solitude. But for all that he was an honest soul, and his daughter-in-law Charlotte called him a remarkable and gifted man who retained his mental powers to the last.

Elisabeth Dorothea is reported to have been very happy as

* His country seat.

a child and young girl, but her experience of life – the loss of her father's fortune, her husband's prolonged absences, the death of two small children – lent her character a seriousness that was deep though never anything but courageous. 'Our dear mother,' writes Christophine, 'seems to feed on constant worry. If she can no longer find it in one place, she painfully seeks it in another.' Her belief in God has been described as possessing a 'mystical' quality; but it should not be forgotten that our informants lived at the time of the Enlightenment,* and that consequently the mysticism of which they speak probably only means that the well-springs of her faith lay deeper than human reason could penetrate.

Poets get their poetry from their mothers, a fact which is quite clear in Schiller's case too. He was like his mother, too, in that seriousness predominated just as strongly, and yet there always remained in his memory the gaiety and the delight in games that he enjoyed as a child. It was to blossom again in the days of his maturity, and provide the most moving moment in the story of his life. It is then (1800) that he sings the praises of his mother in his *Lied von der Glocke* (*Song of the Bell*) – and she lived to hear them. Could they be sung with greater solemnity than he sings them?

Die Räume wachsen, es dehnt sich das Haus.
Und drinnen waltet
Die züchtige Hausfrau,
Die Mutter der Kinder,
Und herrschet weise
Im häuslichen Kreise
Und lehret die Mädchen
Und wehret den Knaben
Und reget ohn Ende
Die fleißigen Hände
Und mehrt den Gewinn
Mit ordnendem Sinn,
Und füllet mit Schätzen den duftenden Laden
Und dreht um die schnurrende Spindel den Faden

* See below, p. 38.

Und sammelt im reinlich geglätteten Schrein
Die schimmernde Wolle, den schneeigten Lein
Und füget zum Guten den Glanz und den Schimmer
Und ruhet nimmer.*

It was a great blow to Frau Schiller when Friedrich fled from Württemberg (in 1781 when he was twenty-two) and had for many years to live precariously in exile.† A malignant stomach complaint attacked her, which was undoubtedly caused by worrying about her son and the impossibility of helping him. The doctors were unable to help her, and it was her own constitution, which had great vitality in spite of being delicate, that finally threw it off. In later years her greatest source of comfort was her son's astronomical rise to fame, and, even more than that, his constant and faithful concern for her, no matter how far they might be apart. She was happy to be able to tell her friends and visitors that no one ever had a better son than she. Soon after his marriage (1790) he had invited her to live with them in Jena; when he visited his Swabian home in 1793, she saw the birth of her first grandson and, wearing her black church-going dress, bore him proudly in her arms to the font. When, around the middle of the 1790's, the French war once again swept across southern Germany, the women had to hide in cellars and caves from the marauding French soldiery who forced their way into houses. The Solitude became a hospital and an epidemic broke out there. Frau Schiller wore herself out nursing her husband and her youngest daughter. Nanette died of the disease which the invasion brought with it, and Kaspar Schiller soon followed her.

Schiller's mother spent her last years with her daughter Luise, and after the latter's marriage lived alone in Leonberg

* The rooms increase, the house expands. And within, the chaste housewife is active, the children's mother, and rules wisely in the domestic circle, and teaches the girls and restrains the boys, and ceaselessly works with her busy hands, and increases the earnings with her orderly mind, and fills the fragrant chests with treasures, and winds the thread on the humming spindle, and piles into the cupboard, clean and polished, the shimmering wool and the snowy linen, and adds shine and shimmer to all that is good, and never rests.

† See Chapter III, p. 57.

Castle, where she had been assigned widow's quarters. She busied herself doing things to help her children and kept her son's household in the 'snowy linen' which she wove herself. Luise's husband was the pastor of Cleversulzbach, and Luise had her mother brought there when she fell fatally ill; it was there that she died peacefully in the spring of 1802, and there too she was buried. 'See the sunken hillock,' says Mörike's* poem written more than thirty years later, when he too was pastor of Cleversulzbach, 'See the sunken hillock, the oldest in the village scarcely know it any longer, and nobody guesses that something sacred is here. . . . Wild rose! you alone do I find in place of other flowers; that's right, shame them, break forth like a miracle! . . . The mother of an immortal lies buried here.' It was Mörike, too, who had a gravestone raised to her and buried his own mother beside her.

Lorch on the Rems: a valley enclosed by dark, fir-covered slopes, a more severe and mysterious place than Marbach, but with better communications to the outside world, for the main road from Stuttgart to Nuremberg passes through the village. To the south there is a distant view of the Rauhe Alb,† to the west the hazy blue of wooded heights. This was the country of Schiller's childhood, where he awoke to consciousness of nature and the world around him. Together with his sister Christophine, who late in life still remembered their days in Lorch as a time 'when we were so marvellously happy', he roamed the woods, or else they climbed the Liebfrauenberg to the monastery of Lorch with its cloister and ancient linden-tree, and stood by the graves of the Hohenstaufen dynasty.‡ There was some-

---

* Eduard Mörike (1804–75), a fellow-Swabian, one of Germany's greatest lyric poets, was trained as a Lutheran pastor and held the living of Cleversulzbach from 1834–44, when he retired for reasons of health.

† The central part (up to 3,000 ft. high) of the Swabian range to the west of Ulm.

‡ A Swabian dynasty, German Emperors from 1138–1254. Conradin, the last of the line, was executed (aged sixteen) at Naples in 1268, having been captured on an expedition to Italy by Charles of Anjou. Himself a minor minnesinger, he became for contemporary and subsequent poets a romantic symbol of doomed youth.

thing special about the linden-tree. It was old enough to have seen the age of the Hohenstaufen rulers; and its main branch was broken by a storm on November 1, 1755, the same night on which Lisbon was destroyed by an earthquake, an event which was interpreted, in that windless season, as a dreadful warning. So the place held for the children a thrill of mystery, part natural, part historical. Today the linden-tree is no longer there. It was already damaged, and in a stormy winter's night in 1955 it was destroyed utterly. In the nave of the monastery church there stands a sarcophagus bearing the Hohenstaufen coat of arms, and the rulers' portraits are painted on the piers. In Schiller's day they were faded and almost obliterated, but in the 1880's they were restored to their former colour and distinctness. In one of them one can see Conradin, destined to die young, and the scene of his execution. A play on the subject of Conradin was one of Schiller's earliest dramatic plans. In it he would doubtless not have sung the mythical Southern Kingdom of the Germans; it would probably have assumed some such shape as did later the story of Don Carlos, a prince who sets out to realize 'the bold vision of a new state'.

The children attended the village school in Lorch which, under the headmaster of the day, was not exactly a model of what such institutions should be. But the village possessed a pastor, Philipp Ulrich Moser, who came from the school of Johann Albrecht Bengel, a theologian prominent in the field of scriptural exegesis; he was himself a learned theologian and, even more important, an upright man. Young Friedrich, to whom Moser taught Latin together with his own son at an astonishingly early age, commemorated him subsequently in *Die Räuber* (*The Robbers*)* in the figure of the courageous pastor who opposes the unbeliever and man of violence, Franz Moor. Moser became Schiller's boyhood hero and he wanted to become a pastor himself, which made his mother very happy. He made her give him a cap and tie a black apron round him;

---

* Schiller's first play (1780). See Chapters II and III.

he then preached sermons with great solemnity, and became very angry if anyone laughed at him.

A clerical vocation seemed such an obvious choice in those days for any pupil whose interests tended at all towards the world of humane studies, that the family really seem from that time on to have viewed their son as a future pastor. When, at the end of 1766 – i.e. when Friedrich was barely seven – Captain Schiller was transferred from Lorch to Ludwigsburg, he put him at once into the 'Latin School' (*Lateinschule*), where not only was Latin taught, but no other subject was taught at all except on Fridays, which were devoted to the study of German. It was in fact a preparatory school for theological studies, and at fourteen, after the annual state examinations, its pupils entered a seminary, from which they went directly into curacies.

So the world of childhood was soon past, and perhaps for that very reason it remained for Schiller a realm of tender, inviolable memories. No more village and green-shaded river, but instead Ludwigsburg, a town with long, broad streets, where many people were to be seen walking about, and tall urban houses. But the lessons with Pastor Moser had been thorough, and he passed the Latin entrance examination without any trouble. In the lodgings right next door lived a family, von Hoven by name, who had a boy of Schiller's age, Wilhelm. Wilhelm became his school-companion and friend.

Wilhelm von Hoven was also to remain his close companion later on, during the time they spent in the Karl Eugen school,* but first they spent six years together at school in Ludwigsburg. They shared the annual examination fears and made enthusiastic plans for the future as boys do; they also both admired their chief preceptor, Jahn, whose pupils did not have an easy time but nevertheless enjoyed being taught by him. There is no direct evidence that Schiller had any difficulties with the Lutheran orthodoxy of the institution, but that such was the case emerges all the more clearly from the severity with which, in later life, he criticized the Christian doctrine of

---

* The *Karlsschule*, see below, pp. 28-43.

Original Sin, and even disapproved Kant's recognition of radical evil. The hidebound theologians of the eighteenth century only managed to depict Original Sin to Schiller and his contemporaries as a scourge, not as a necessary presupposition of that primal liberty of mankind which reaches back to the Garden of Eden, and so they prevented them from grasping this basic insight of the Christian faith. If Schiller clung to the idea of his clerical vocation, it was only in the pietist sense, which has its roots in the family and the prayerful devotion of the individual. The writer Hermann Kurz relates how a pastor was once asked in company what a pietist was. He asked in return: 'What does your dog do, sir, if you keep on beating him?' 'He looks for a kinder master.' 'Now observe: everyone beats the common people – the duke, the soldiers, the game-keepers, the parsons. So finally they run away and seek another master with whom they will be better off. This master is Christ, and he who seeks Christ is a pietist.'

The town of Ludwigsburg was at that time a Residency (state capital), because the Duke – at loggerheads with his Diet who did not submit to his despotic rule without some slight show of resistance – had angrily withdrawn from Stuttgart and now reigned and resided at his country seat, The Solitude, which had only recently (1767) been completed. His household included latterly a school for the future officers and officials of his State. It was first of all called the military academy, and later the *Karlsschule*.* The court entertainments – Italian operas and French plays, ballets and tightrope-walkers, and during carnival time the Venetian Fair, which even ordinary subjects were allowed to attend in masks – also moved to Ludwigsburg and The Solitude. Of course, respectable citizens shunned the court as a sink of iniquity, and those with pretty daughters certainly had every reason not to expose them to the appetites (which often took violent forms) of the ruling classes. But the young people could not be prevented from looking on at the festive pageants and performances, least of all by one who, like

* Literally: 'Karl's School', i.e. the school of Karl Eugen.

26

Captain Schiller, was in the ducal service. We can be sure that in his household strict silence was observed on matters concerning the background to court life, and that Friedrich learned nothing about it for many years, except for rumours of which he would scarcely have comprehended very much.

When he was thirteen, in 1772, Schiller prepared for his confirmation. On the day before his mother saw him romping carefree in the street. Horrified, she called him to her and reproached him for his frivolity, and urgently admonished him to reflect on the significance of the coming day. Whereupon Schiller, as he himself related to a friend in later years, went to his room, from which he emerged after a while with a religious poem. If his memory is correct – the poem has not been preserved – then the incident demonstrates how tightly the parental world still enclosed him as a schoolboy, and how complete was his acceptance of its standards and directions.

That was shortly before Duke Karl Eugen intervened personally in his young subject's life.

CHAPTER II

THE KARLSSCHULE
(1773-80)

*

An absolute ruler in a small state makes everything his concern. Reports of the State Examinations had to be submitted to the Duke, and from them he learned which pupils were gifted and which were dunderheads. He noticed that the son of his Captain Schiller had a good brain, that he was just about to take his final examination and that he would enter a religious seminary in the autumn of 1773. He sent for the father and offered to have his son educated in his academy, whereupon Captain Schiller replied that from his earliest youth his son had cherished an inclination for the religious life, and if he could continue to develop this inclination in the institution, he would esteem it a favour if his son were accepted; a polite and careful way of saying no, for it was clear that the Catholic Duke did not train up theologians for his Protestant Estates in his school. Karl Eugen seems, too, to have replied at first that he had no use for a cleric as a pupil in his academy. There were some grounds for hoping that the dreaded favour had happily passed by. But then the Duke twice repeated his offer that Friedrich Schiller should be sent to his academy, 'where the choice of studies would be left to him, and on leaving he would provide for him better than would be possible in the clerical profession'. The whole thing was still being done very graciously, for instead of making offers he could quite simply command, and had already done so in similar cases without more ado. The control over his subjects' children was for him only a normal part of his all-embracing rights. None could doubt that the family would run into serious danger if the ruler's thrice-repeated offer were declined. So they had to submit. Even Friedrich, it is said, consented, chiefly out of consideration for his parents, though 'tormented in spirit'.

It was in such dramatic circumstances that Schiller first made the acquaintance of his sovereign, and found himself handed over as material for the latter's pedagogical experiments. What sort of man was it into whose hands he had fallen?

During the age of the Enlightenment even the physiognomy of men in power shows a somewhat more elevated trait, whereas so many of them had previously looked as if they did nothing but drink and fight. There is no doubt that, for princes, an era of new responsibility had dawned. The well-known woodcut of Duke Karl Eugen reveals a face neither ignoble nor lacking in intellect. Brow, eyes and nose are all good, with a trace of sensuality and mockery around the mouth, but not of a repulsive kind.

The names of his two predecessors on the ducal throne, Eberhard Ludwig and Karl Alexander, are connected with those of the courtesan Grävenitz and the exploiter, Jew Süss: the country preserved bitter memories of those days. When Karl Alexander died, his son was only nine years old, and the land revived under a regency. Karl Eugen spent some of his early years at the court of Frederick the Great, who had a good opinion of his capabilities. However, Frederick did no service to the people of Württemberg when he helped to enforce the premature declaration of the Duke's majority. He married him off to his niece, Friderike of Bayreuth. At first she exercised a moderating influence on the Duke, but his nature was unable to resist the temptation to do and have whatever he pleased. When he took a French singer as his mistress, Friderike climbed into her travelling-coach and went home to Bayreuth. From that day there were no more restraints on Karl Eugen. Ostentation, building-mania, herds of game for his hunt which no peasant was allowed to touch when they ruined fields and vineyards, and in addition a harem of Italian and local women which the Duke had travelling behind him in a train of coaches when on his journeys – all these things consumed the country's wealth and at the same time were as ridiculous as they were immoral. He was a German village tyrant who aped the Sun King* and could treat his subjects according to how the fancy took him. That he sold them for military service against his patron Frederick of Prussia is a fact which has already been mentioned. Moreover, official posts in the land were sold to the highest bidder, and lucrative new taxes were devised and gathered. It was this system, as run by the Duke's favourites Montmartin, Rieger and Wittleder, against which the Parliament finally lodged a complaint with the Emperor, appealing to the ancient constitution of Württemberg; and justice was done them. The Duke was obliged to dismiss the offenders and promise, in the so-called *Erbvergleich*† of 1770, to restore the injured constitution. The question arises: did Karl Eugen merely bow to the inevitable, or was he really ashamed of his previous behaviour, did he undergo an inner conversion to what was right and proper? One may feel sure that the woman who came into his life at this time, Franziska von Leutrum, whom he later created Countess Hohenheim, did her best to impress upon him a sense of his responsibilities as a ruler. He was not able to marry her until 1785, after the death of Friderike, but Franziska's grace and intelligence, and her gentle hand, became a source of blessing for the sorely-tried people. Something of this still shines through in the figure of Schiller's Lady Milford (in *Kabale und Liebe*), a clear reflection of her character. The education of young people now became Karl Eugen's special hobby. There may have been a good deal of playful vanity in the way he showed off his pupils, whom he called his 'sons', a fact which earned for him the mocking lines of the poet Schubart:

* Karl Eugen was an extreme, but by no means untypical, example of the habit of many German rulers of the day of modelling their courts on Louis XIV's Versailles: see A. Fauchier-Magnan, *The Small German Courts in the 18th Century.*

† A settlement of claims to an inheritance.

Als Dionys von Syrakus
Aufhören mußt, Tyrann zu sein,
Da ward er ein Schulmeisterlein.*

But he made his academy into a good school, chiefly by
employing outstanding teachers. Jahn, the Ludwigsburg preceptor, taught there for several years, and we shall hear later
about Magister Abel. The whole of Germany was interested
in the *Karlsschule*; it was visited not only by Karl August of
Saxony-Weimar, but also by the Emperor Joseph II, and the
latter raised it in 1781 to the rank of an academy. While it is
certain that Karl Eugen wanted only the best for his pupils, it
is equally certain that he was only ever able to conceive that
best in his own peculiar way. And complaints were still heard
about the continuing traffic in offices and the over-numerous
herds of game, nor were pretty girls safe from their sovereign's
favour; his excuse in this last matter is worth noting: it no
longer afforded him any pleasure, but it was a habit, like
tobacco.

The most unjust of his acts is certainly his treatment of
Schubart, whose well-aimed shaft he had been unable to
forget. Christian Friedrich Daniel Schubart (1739–91) was
something of a genius with a vein of genuine poetry in him,
careless, however, not only with wine and no doubt with
women too, but, more dangerously, with tongue and pen. First
of all he quarrelled with the Württemberg clergy and was
banished from the country; then he edited a paper in Ulm
which served as a quiver from which to shoot his arrows of
mockery. Early in 1777 Duke Karl Eugen had him enticed to
Blaubeuren by one Scholl, a high-bailiff, from where he was
taken to fortress-arrest at Hohenasperg. He spent a year in a
dark vault without any means of occupying himself. Then
relaxations were granted, and attempts were made to improve
his sense of a subject's duties. Schubart never learned the reason
for his captivity, nor did he receive a sentence. When, after

* 'When Dionysus of Syracuse had to stop being a tyrant, he became a little
schoolmaster.'

Religion ist (dem Inhalte nach) kein Unterschied aller Pflichten als göttlicher Gebote...

[handwritten inscription — partially legible]

Immanuel Kant (1791)

3. Immanuel Kant. Engraving by Karl Barth after a drawing by Stobbe

to the Duke. It appears that, in the event, permission was in fact granted on compassionate grounds. But such conditions make it appear likely that that other tale is not an invention which relates how the Duke, in a similar case, refused a pupil permission to visit his dying father, and had the effrontery to console the weeping lad with the words: 'Be quiet: I will be your father.' The whole institution, in fact, was based on such compulsory 'fatherhood'. For that reason the pupils were only permitted brief and infrequent visits from their relatives, and never without a previous petition to the Duke; moreover, a superintendent had to be present during the conversation. The pupil's correspondence was supervised, in fact rewards were given for informing on letters secretly smuggled out of the school. However highly one may rate the academic attainments of the academy, one is forced to admit that the place was a prison.

But even worse, as it seems to us, than the physical was the mental compulsion which made the pupils, on the Duke's own birthdays and those of his Countess Franziska, compose flattering speeches in prose and verse. It is not pleasant to have to read the following from Schiller's pen: 'I see before me the father of my parents, whose graciousness I can never repay. I behold him, and sigh. This prince, who has made it possible for my parents to do good to me, this prince, through whom God will achieve his purpose for me, this father, who desires to make me happy, is and must be more estimable to me than my parents, who utterly depend on his favour. Could I but approach him with the gratitude which ecstasy wrings from me,' etc. But we would do well to realize that these, and all subsequent stylistic exercises in the language of the courtier which have survived from Schiller's school days, had no power to sap the vitality of a young and vigorous will, provided that the community could offer other opportunities for the development of mind and character. It appears certain to me that Schiller and his friends thought about and performed these things with as little mental damage to themselves as they did the dressing-up for midday meals. They rose at six o'clock (five in the summer), ate their breakfast porridge and had lessons from seven till eleven, and then were obliged to pull on their steel-blue coat with silver buttons, white waistcoat and white trousers; a rolled pigtail formed an important part of the costume, as did a black three-cornered hat with silver braid and cockade, a sword and top-boots. Thus they marched into the marshalling-hall, formed up in ranks and were inspected, praised or criticized, mostly by the Duke himself, who attended the midday and evening meals nearly every day. Then they marched into the dining-hall, said grace at a word of command and received a simple but plentiful meal consisting of soup, meat and vegetables, sometimes followed by pastries. There was a leisure hour in the garden until two o'clock, then lessons (not homework) until seven, followed once more by dressing up in their best uniform and a meal. Bedtime was at nine o'clock, and no one was allowed to be up after that. They hung their uniforms up in the cupboard and thought as little of them as of the parade of flattery in their exercises.

As there was soon not enough room at The Solitude, the Residency and the academy were transferred to Stuttgart, and the new home of the *Karlsschule* was the barracks behind the ducal palace. In military order, with their superiors and teachers, and with Karl Eugen riding on horseback at their head, the pupils entered Stuttgart on November 18, 1775; the people welcomed them with joy: it was a solemn reconciliation between the Duke and his capital. A medical department was added to the academy, and the pupils were called upon to volunteer for it. Schiller and Hoven both declared themselves ready for the new course of studies: they seem to have won but little glory in law, which they had been studying up till then.

However, it was not medicine, but poetry which gradually reconciled Schiller with his lot: one imagines it as a brightly-coloured spirit-bird flying in at the window. He still cherished an affection from home for the songs of the poet Gellert,* which

---

* Christian Fürchtegott Gellert (1715–69), Professor of Poetry, Rhetoric and

seemed like a soft echo of childhood. But now during the early days in the *Karlsschule*, later but with a more passionate reaction than many contemporaries, he discovered Klopstock.* 'Sing, immortal soul, the redemption of sinful humanity. . . .' When the characteristic line of *Der Messias* (*The Messiah*) first rang out, flowing like rays of light or waves of the sea, the genius of the German language spoke anew, and the genius of the nation that speaks through that language. The tongue with which the new literature spoke – that of Goethe, Schiller, Hölderlin† and Jean Paul‡ was unloosed by Klopstock. Then, too, the poetic word accomplished that strange and continually incomprehensible thing: it hollowed out a space in what, in this case, was really emptiness, a space which the spirit of the nation could inhabit. Here we have a great people and a great country, ravaged by The Thirty Years War (1618–48), and since then split up into autonomous states, almost devoid of spiritual self-awareness and without the sense of a common culture: and then a poet arises, he scarcely seems to know what he is doing and who is listening to him, but suddenly meaning, language and

---

Moral Philosophy at Leipzig, celebrated as a poet and writer of stories and comedies, chiefly famous for his novel *The Swedish Countess* (1746), but whose songs were loved in German homes for two centuries.

* Friedrich Gottlieb Klopstock (1724–1803), a pietistically-inclined epic and lyric poet. His ambition was to provide a German equivalent of Milton's *Paradise Lost*. The result was *Der Messias*, a hexameter epic in twenty cantos which established him as the leading poet of the day and laid the foundation of the renascence of German as an instrument of poetry. Klopstock, who is also celebrated for his odes, became the focus of the cult of sensibility (*Empfindsamkeit*) which was a feature of German personal relationships during the remainder of the century.

† Friedrich Hölderlin (1770–1843), also a Swabian, one of the greatest of German lyric poets. His elevated conception of the nature of poetry and the poet's mission link him with the Romantic movement, whilst his cult of Hellenism and his blending of Christian themes with the ideals of a (largely imaginary) Classical Antiquity are connected with the Classicism of Goethe and Schiller. For the last forty years of his life he was insane.

‡ Johann Paul Friedrich Richter (1763–1825), whose admiration for Rousseau led him to adopt the pen-name of Jean Paul, was the most famous novelist of his age. Neither a Classicist nor a Romantic, despite affinities with both trends, his blend of idealism and robustly fantastical inventiveness make his descriptions of the whole range of German life, and in particular his genre-painting, one of the most characteristic expressions of the German genius.

resonance are there. (The myth relates that Echo was a mountain-spirit and friendly with the highest of the gods.) Such was the event in the history of German thought which bears the name of Klopstock. And it is significant that once again, as in the age when *Der Heliand* (*The Saviour*)* was written, this event stood under the sign of the Christian dispensation. That was the spring from which ground and roots were watered, whatever horticultural feats the poets might perform. J. W. Petersen, a fellow pupil and friend of Schiller's, has affirmed that the latter's preoccupation with Klopstock was no brief nibble at a toothsome morsel: he calls it 'a serious, daily, continuing process of attention, feeling, contemplation, comparison, research and appropriation. It is an indisputable fact that this warm-hearted and total absorbing of Klopstock's views . . . had a pronounced effect upon Schiller's education'. His first attempts at verse are evidence of that – *Hymne an den Unendlichen* (*Hymn to the Infinite*), *An die Sonne* (*To the Sun*), *Der Eroberer* (*The Conqueror*) – attempts which, although echoing Klopstock, show him to be more than just the latter's pupil; it was in these poems, in fact, that he awoke to his own poetic vocation.

Yet this impulse was to be received with scornful suspicion by the fellow-pupil he had chosen above all others to be his friend: Scharffenstein. 'O, a friendship such as this one,' Schiller wrote to him, 'could have lasted through all eternity!' Like everyone else in those days, the inmates of the *Karlsschule* were prone to 'enthusiasm'. It was Jean-Jacques Rousseau's faith in nature and humanity which caused this inner uprising; there was a cult of friendship which no doubt led to many eccentricities, but also produced much that was fine. The readiness to view great things greatly and to acknowledge and surrender oneself to absolutes ran like a leaping fire through the veins of that generation. But Scharffenstein had reproached him – and he held fast to his extremely unjust verdict during Schiller's later life as well – with being less concerned with the heart than

---

* *Der Heliand*: a 6,000-line epic poem (author unknown) of about 830 A.D·which transfers the life of Christ to a Saxon setting.

with the laurels he could win; his enthusiasm was mere poetry culled from Klopstock, he lacked a serious concern for humanity. This is a warning which every idealistically-inclined temperament prone to impatient disregard of human limitations must be prepared to hear. One can see from the tone, more sorrowful than angry, of the letter which the poet wrote to Scharffenstein how painfully it affected him, and one can still catch an echo of it in *Die Räuber*, when the robbers say to Karl Moor: 'Let him go. It's megalomania. He wants to risk his life just to win admiration.' But Schiller nevertheless defends Klopstock, and in most serious terms: 'Admittedly I owe a great deal to Klopstock, but it has sunk deep into my soul and become my own inmost feeling, my own property; and this is true; this can comfort me in death.'

It is because of this that Schiller always honoured the genius who inspired his youth, although in a retrospective essay of 1795 he says that no poet is less suited to be a companion throughout life than Klopstock – 'who is always leading us away from life, is always calling the spirit to arms, without providing refreshment for the mind by means of a concrete external reality'. This was the next artistic experience he was to meet, through Goethe, whose *Werther* (and, earlier, whose *Goetz*)* had depicted nature with a power and innocence quite new to the age. It was over *Goetz* that the divining-rod of Schiller's dramatic imagination gave its most vigorous twitch. He later appeared himself in the title rôle of Goethe's *Clavigo* (1774) in a performance at the *Karlsschule*, not a particularly

* *Goetz von Berlichingen* (1773), a dramatization of the life of a sixteenth-century robber-baron, and *Die Leiden des jungen Werthers* (1774), a novel in letter-form describing the hopeless love and suicide of a sensitive, nature-loving young man, were two of the works which established the fame of Johann Wolfgang von Goethe (1749–1832), who, as lyric-poet, playwright, novelist and thinker is the dominant figure in German literary and cultural history. With *Goetz* he initiated, under the influence of Johann Gottfried Herder (1744–1803), the movement of revolt (*Sturm und Drang*) against the domination of life and literature by Enlightenment rationalism, but himself moved on to a more balanced view of life based on his guiding principle which saw nature, man and art as forming an organic whole subject to growth and development. His experience of human problems as a Minister of State in the small Duchy of Weimar, his

happy one, according to reports: he was not gifted as an actor. Lessing's* *Emilia Galotti* had appeared as early as 1772, but much as Schiller admired it and was to learn from it, the writers of the *Sturm und Drang (Storm and Stress)* movement were closer to him.

[This literary movement, which took its name from the sub-title of a play by Friedrich Maximilian von Klinger (1752–1831), represented a reaction against the domination by Enlightenment Rationalism of all branches of German intellectual, social and literary life. Its protagonists – of whom the most important, after Goethe, were his friends and associates Klinger, Reinhold Lenz (1751–92), Johann Anton Leisewitz (1752–1806) and Friedrich ('Maler') Müller (1749–1825) – absorbed ideas from a variety of sources. From Johann Georg Hamann (1730-88) and his pupil Johann Gottfried Herder (1744–1803) they learned to distrust the flat formulations of speculative reason and to seek a more reliable contact with reality through the life of the emotions and the poetic intuitions of unsophisticated peoples; from Rousseau they acquired a similar preference for the irrational and an impatience with the corruption of the established social structure; Shakespeare taught them that dramatic literature should be a reflection of the totality of human experience: for them he represented 'Natur' – their watchword. Their

---

protracted and wide-ranging scientific studies, the moderating influence of his love for Charlotte von Stein, a lady of the Weimar court, and the impact of his visit to Italy and the art and thought of Classical Antiquity, combined to produce a humane ideal of the total and harmonious development of all man's faculties, an ideal reflected in such plays as *Iphigenia auf Tauris* (1787) and *Torquato Tasso* (1789) and the novels *Wilhelm Meister* (1795–96) and *Die Wahlverwandtschaften* (*The Elective Affinities*) (1809). But perhaps his most characteristic work is *Faust*, a play in two parts at which he worked for sixty years and in which he depicts the struggle and ultimate triumph of the human spirit in its quest for power and self-knowledge.

* Gotthold Ephraim Lessing (1729–81) was the leading spirit of the Enlightenment in German literature, equally distinguished as a playwright and a critic. He himself never laid claim to great creative ability, but his plays, based on his own close contacts with the theatre, provided admirable models of dramatic construction, as well as possessing intrinsic merits which have enabled them to hold their own on the German stage to this day. As a critic, aesthetician and thinker Lessing was both a pioneer and a model.

ideas were expressed almost exclusively in dramatic form, in which Heinrich von Gerstenberg (1737–1823) with his *Ugolino* (1768) may be viewed as their precursor. Their aspirations exceeded their achievements. With the exception of Goethe's and Schiller's *Sturm und Drang* works, which may be considered to open and conclude the movement respectively, their products, with their crudeness of language, violence of feeling and general formlessness (which frequently derived from a misguided imitation of Shakespeare) are mainly interesting now as literary-historical documents, despite the flashes of original genius these young men sometimes revealed.]*

Finally Shakespeare fell into Schiller's hand. He has related himself what difficulties he had with him at first in his youthful enthusiasm: 'I was indignant at his coldness, his lack of sensitivity, which permitted him to jest at moments of emotional crisis, to interrupt the heartbreaking scenes in *Lear*, *Hamlet* and *Macbeth* with the entry of a Fool, at one moment to pause when my own feelings hurried on, and at the next to plunge on when the heart would gladly have lingered.' Schiller adds: 'I was not yet capable of comprehending nature at first hand.' But for all that, Shakespeare ousted all other poets from Schiller's mind for a considerable space of time; for years on end he wooed and wrestled with his great model, to set up finally a dramatic form of his own which possessed a much greater independence and validity than his critic Otto Ludwig† was ever able to grasp with his bookish burrowings. The first daring product of this struggle was *Die Räuber*. He was caught reading Shakespeare by a supervisor; as the book was not among those officially permitted, it was taken from him. Magister Abel returned it to him, and thus began an important friendship.

Like Schiller himself and his comrade Hoven, Jakob Fried-

* Translator's interpolation.
† Otto Ludwig (1813–65), German playwright, story-writer and critic; he disapproved of Schiller, spending many years studying Shakespeare in order to deduce valid dramatic principles from him, and was himself one of the chief theorists and practitioners of the movement of Poetic Realism in nineteenth-century German literature.

rich Abel had been intended for the church when Duke Karl
Eugen intervened and installed him (he was just about to be
ordained) as a master in his school. He had shown himself a
shrewd judge of character. Abel was a small man, gentle and
inconspicuous, but possessing a firmness of character which
the Duke himself came to be aware of where justice in school
affairs was concerned, and considerable pedagogic talent. It is
reported of his teaching that he did not deliver a systematic
scheme in the usual sense of concepts derived from primary
principles, but encouraged his pupils to co-operate with him
by enquiring after their own observations and experiences,
upon which the sought-for concepts and general laws were then
built up. It was through his influence that philosophy was made
a main subject at the *Karlsschule*. Abel was born in 1751, and
thus, like other teachers in the academy incidentally, so close in
age to the pupils that a relationship of mutual trust arose between scholars and instructors, and many dangerous situations
in the absolutist system of education were counteracted. 'The
pupil,' wrote Abel himself, 'communicated his most important
secrets to the teacher and asked his advice in matters which
normally are more carefully concealed from teachers and
superiors than from anyone else.'

Schiller seems to have inhabited an idealistic and sensitive
world of his own, isolated in the midst of the school community, but from his seventeenth year on, a perceptible change
in his life seems to have occurred, and it was Abel who helped
him to thrust open the door. Just as, in his teaching, Abel took
the experience of the individual as his starting-point, so in
conversation he doubtless pointed out to Schiller, who was
given to high-flown speculation, that the human mind is housed
in a very limited and contingent body. And he must similarly
have shown at the same time that medical studies, which for
Schiller were merely an irksome scholastic duty, also possessed
meaning and importance. It is reported that Schiller now completely renounced poetry for a time, until he caught up on his
neglected medical studies; he persevered in his determination

and attained his goal. Abel was a theologian, but he lived, breathed and thought in an age which claimed nature and reason as its great discoveries; and if it is true that contemporaneity should be viewed as a mission and a destiny, then he owed it to his pupils and to himself not to avoid a frank discussion of such problems. Schiller felt it to be a challenge that the soul should be dependent on the body, and the mind determined by the chance operation of external causes. This view overreaches itself in the materialist speculations of Franz Moor ('Man issues from mud and lives in a muddy ferment'), but is objectivized by being allotted to the villain. Schiller's innate conviction that it is 'the spirit which constructs the body for itself' breaks through. It was the Scotsman Thomas Reid who expressed the thought that there was an 'inner light' in man which was a gift of nature, and just as much a fact of experience as any communicated by the senses. This opinion was also to be found in Reid's pupil Ferguson and in the German translation and interpretation of the latter's works by Christian Garve, where Schiller became acquainted with it and found his own view profoundly and gratefully confirmed. For it was not merely his own world of 'ideality' which was thus saved; a courageous spirit measuring for the first time the full spread of its wings perceived that the comprehension of human nature in its entirety was the goal that it, too, had been set. Goethe, when, in old age, he came to speak about his relationship with Schiller, frequently intimated that he felt himself to be a kind of messenger sent by nature in order to reconcile him with her. If one is willing to accept that, then the teacher of his youth, Abel, was the first of her messengers. On December 12, 1779, Goethe himself, returning home from Switzerland as the travelling companion of Karl August, visited the *Karlsschule* and attended a formal prize-giving. A lanky, red-haired, clumsy fellow with the pale, tense face of an intellectual received three prizes for medicine; he was not the type to attract Goethe's friendly notice, and others received prizes as well. The author of *Werther*, the object of three hundred young people's awed admiration, had no way of knowing that this was the one amongst them who was destined to be his friend, a companion on lofty paths which he had resigned himself to travelling alone.

Schiller had counted on leaving the *Karlsschule* at the end of that year; he was twenty now, and justifiably impatient to be out in the world. His final dissertation bore the title *Philosophie der Physiologie* (*The Philosophy of Physiology*), and in it he had spoken his mind and heart without reserve. For that reason the Duke found it unsuitable for publication and decided that Schiller should spend a further year in the academy, 'during which time his ardour may be cooled somewhat, so that he may then, if he remains diligent, assuredly become a considerable fellow'. It is as if the fowler knew that he would no longer be able to keep the bird once the cage door was open. The action was not completely arbitrary, in so far as the question of admitting medical students from the academy to practice had not been fully negotiated with the State medical authorities, so that the Duke would not immediately have been able to make good his promise to look after them; but there is no doubt that Schiller felt bitter about the year's postponement.

It was now that *Die Räuber*, which had, of course, been sketched and begun much earlier, came to fruition. At about the same time the early work *Semele, a lyrical operetta in two scenes* must have been written as well, a more important work than its author was willing to admit in his maturity. It was important, not merely because it points forward thematically (Semele, the beloved of Zeus, is a mortal to whom her love proves fatal because of the jealousy of Juno) to Kleist's* dramatic myth *Amphitryon* and to Hölderlin's hymn *Das himmlische Feuer* (*The Heavenly Fire*), but also as evidence of the young Schiller's

---

* Bernd Heinrich Wilhelm von Kleist (1777–1811), a Prussian officer turned writer, one of the most powerful tragic dramatists of the Romantic age, and as a writer of short stories one of the chief formative influences on the genre in the nineteenth century. His studies in Kantian and Romantic philosophy reacted with an unstable temperament to produce, on the one hand, literary works of unparalleled terseness and tragic impact, and, on the other, an inability to cope with the practical problems of life which led him to shoot himself at the age of thirty-three.

already fully-developed power of poetic expression. This semi-lyric entertainment, in which there are nevertheless strong dramatic undertones, can only be seen in its proper perspective if placed beside its larger sibling, *Die Räuber*. These two represent the break-through, the decisive poetic product of Schiller's years of waiting. In the pupils' rooms there was no light of an evening. Schiller reported sick, because he could use the lamp in the sick-bay to write by. If a supervisor or even the Duke himself appeared unexpectedly, the papers disappeared beneath a medical textbook. For he could not let himself be caught writing poetry, 'an inclination for poetry infringed the laws of the academy and ran counter to the plan of its founder' . . . thus it is written in the sketch of his life with which Schiller announced his periodical *Rheinische Thalia* (*The Rhenish Thalia*) four years later, from Mannheim. Opportunities were found of secretly reading to his friends what he had written. They were astounded and enthusiastic over it. Schiller announced his express purpose of writing a book 'that would positively have to be burnt by the public hangman'. The younger brother of Wilhelm von Hoven died during that summer, and Schiller composed a *Leichenphantasie* (*Funeral Fantasy*) which reveals the poet in his full panoply. A letter to his friend's father and another to his sister Christophine show him in a very gloomy state of mind. And a report which, as a medical student, he had to make on the state of a pupil's illness revealed more sympathetic penetration of the latter's mental condition than seemed desirable to the superintendent, Herr von Seeger. But these are merely the fluctuations of impetuous youthful energy. He worked at a second dissertation, *Über den Zusammenhang der tierischen Natur des Menschen mit seiner geistigen* (*On the connection between the animal and intellectual natures in man*); this time he took good care not to wear his heart on his sleeve, and submitted a tidy, serviceable piece of examination-work.

When he was released from the *Karlsschule* on December 14, 1780, he took with him the finished manuscript of his play.

CHAPTER III

IN TYRANNOS: *DIE RÄUBER*
(1781-82)

*

Anyone who wishes to make fun of *Die Räuber* can do so easily enough. It is putting it mildly to say that Goethe did not like it: he thought it detestable, and Schiller agreed with him. Later he never wished to see his play performed. Soon after it had been written he thought and spoke very slightingly of it, and in a public review of his own work poked fun at Amalia and Moor senior. The faults are obvious, the clearest being the lack of psychological probability: that human beings should behave and let others behave towards them in such a way.* Karl Moor is studying in Leipzig and has never noticed that his brother at home, the monster Franz, hates him and is trying to turn their father against him. When Franz's letter reaches Saxony to the effect that Karl has been cast off and disinherited by his father on account of his frivolity and debts, Karl does not suspect an intrigue, but, instead, his disappointed trust in his father turns to hatred of the whole heartless and corrupt world. He sets himself up as the captain of a robber band, in order to wage war on an unjust world-order. It is on weak props such as these that the remainder of the action rests. The reader is amazed at the palpable clumsiness of Franz's methods, which a single steady glance, a single sensible word could foil. But then – is it much different in the case of Shakespeare's Iago? Othello stumbles, not over threads, but ropes inches thick. From which the lesson can be learnt that the motivation is much less vital in a drama than the spiritual, human energy which is seen to be

---

* See synopsis, p. 198.

44

set in motion. This power is expressed, in tragedy, in the ability and the readiness to suffer: in pathos, in the original Greek sense of suffering.* Such is the case in Shakespeare, in Calderón and the ancients. It necessarily arises in great drama wherever it is a question of ultimate meaning. This is so in every play by Schiller, but never so openly as in *Die Räuber*. The rascal Franz, who disputes with his servant and Pastor Moser, summoned by night, about the immortality of the soul; the noble Karl, who like Hamlet feels himself born to set right a time which is out of joint, and sees his mission abused and wrecked by the outrages perpetrated by the band of robbers which he commands: both the brothers, just as in medieval and Baroque drama, find themselves directly opposed by the great antagonist, God. Franz dies in despair, Karl submits and acquiesces ('Have mercy on the boy who wished to anticipate thee, for thine alone is the vengeance'). That this antagonist (God) retreats into the background in Schiller's later works, and only acts upon men and their deeds from out of hidden depths, should not mislead us into thinking that he is no longer there and is no longer felt and experienced. In Schiller's first play we smile at the bombastic exaggeration of his characters. But our smile fades as soon as we see them presented in even a moderately tolerable performance, i.e. one in which actors and producer *believe* in them. The demand with which Kleist prefaced his dramas: 'If you believe, then I am for you whatever you would wish, terrible, merry or gentle, just as God wishes. For doubters I sink into nothingness' – this demand must be valid for every poet who thinks decisively, and must always be valid for the dramatist. Then why not for Schiller? If it is fulfilled in his case, then it is utterly impossible to watch the scene previously described, when Franz's letter arrives, Karl reads it, throws it away, runs out, then re-enters, is surrounded by his friends and says: 'Yes, by death with its thousand arms! Robbers and murderers! By my immortal soul, I am your captain!' – it is utterly impossible, I

---

* In German 'Pathos' has the sense of 'stage passion' (very close to 'bombast') and is often applied, sometimes as a reproach, to Schiller's theatrical style.

say, to see this scene without being carried away and ready to
follow this man into the darkest depths of the Bohemian forest.
Or when Karl binds his right hand to the oak-tree and summons his companions to obey the monk's words and take him
prisoner. Schiller wrote irresistible scenes like this in all his
plays; so that, although, for all we may know, a day will come
when people no longer want a living theatre, there can never
be a German theatre without Schiller. A part of this effectiveness is 'Schiller's grandiosity, his delight in a sort of glorified
game of cowboys-and-Indians', which Thomas Mann* spoke
of in his fine commemorative address of 1955, 'the boyishness
and love of adventure which makes such a childish contrast
with his sublimity'. The figure of the intriguer who was to be
his next hero, Fiesko, derives its lustre and driving force from
this quality.

For the moment the young poet's aim was to get his play
into print. He must first of all have breathed a sigh of relief at
being once again with his own people and at his mother's table
after the long separation. Then he had to take up his post. It
was not that of a civilian doctor as he had hoped; he was posted
instead as regimental surgeon to a unit in Stuttgart which con-
sisted for the most part of disabled soldiers. It was certainly
anything but an honourable position, although perhaps the
best the Duke could manage for the moment. Captain Schiller's
petition that his son might be allowed to wear civilian clothes,
so that he might supplement his inadequate income with private
practice, was tersely answered by the Duke: 'Your son must
wear uniform.' Indeed, he required his General's permission
when he wished to leave Stuttgart and visit his family at The
Solitude. Christophine recorded that it was a holiday for the
family when her brother appeared, and his friends can recall
how hospitably his mother received and entertained them when

* One of the last public acts of Thomas Mann (1875–1955), the most distinguished German novelist of the twentieth century, was an address commemo-
rating the 150th anniversary of Schiller's death.

they went out there with him. But such hours were a recreation: the tiresome constraint of army life persisted. And no publisher was willing to risk financing his dramatic monstrosity; Schiller had to have it printed at his own expense; to do this he raised a loan and so laid the foundation of the debts which for years afterwards were to burden and torment him.

When he saw the first proofs, he took fright himself at the wild stuff he had written, and started to alter and tone it down. But even the toned-down version, as soon as it was out, set men's minds on fire. There appeared in Erfurt a review by a novelist of some repute in those days, by name Timme, who straight off made the flat pronouncement: 'If ever we may have hopes of a German Shakespeare, this is he.' In Mannheim the bookseller Schwan, to whom the author had sent his play, went to Heribert Baron von Dalberg, the Director of the National Theatre there (which, after Hamburg, was the most important stage in Germany), and convinced him that this masterpiece had to be performed; the actors saw that the parts offered them golden opportunities such as no other living German play-wright could provide (Lessing had just died, in February 1781). So, in July, Schiller found himself with a letter from Dalberg in which his play was spoken of in very flattering terms, and he was requested to adapt it for the stage, for performance in Mannheim. The letter (which is not extant) seems to have shown an interest in the poet's further productions and to have at least hinted at the possibility of a call to Mannheim. Schiller was young and ingenuous enough to let the other notice his delighted astonishment, and made the mistake – if it was a mistake – of letting himself appear to be the one who was grateful for favours received – which should, of course, have put a large-minded man under an even greater obligation. He let it be seen that he was conscious of the faults in his work. 'But certainly, if ever my powers may rise to the production of a masterpiece, I owe it entirely to Your Excellency's warm commendation, as also does the world at large.'

A short time before, he had gained a young friend, Andreas

Streicher, the son of an artisan's widow, a budding musician. The latter reports from his own experience the impression made by *Die Räuber*, the work of a pupil at the *Karlsschule*, in the placid and inoffensive town of Stuttgart, 'where they nourished their minds only on the pious writings of Gellert, Hagedorn,* Haller,† Klopstock and the like, and where Shakespeare was known to hardly more than a few people. Schiller's name, although his book appeared anonymously, was soon on everyone's lips. Nothing is more understandable than that all sorts of rumours about him were soon current, saying that the Schiller who created the wild robbers was himself of a similar disposition; moreover, Schiller and his comrades, having after years of captivity escaped into academic freedom, will not have missed the opportunity of posing before the respectable citizens of Stuttgart as a public menace. Schiller's regimental commander gave a banquet on the occasion of the Duke's birthday, during which the officers seem to have played a joke on the regimental surgeon, who was only twenty-two but already a local celebrity, and whose lanky, excessively thin figure looked very comic in its stiff uniform: they decided to drink him under the table. They succeeded, and Schiller had to be carried home in a litter. 'From that day on,' reports Abel, who was perturbed by his pupil's bad reputation and investigated the facts, 'the tale was generally believed that he was in the habit of getting drunk'.

What his everyday life in Stuttgart was really like, is well described by Scharffenstein, with whom he had renewed his friendship about this time: 'Schiller lived in a little ground-floor room with Lieutenant Kapf, who had come from the academy with him. We were poor (Scharffenstein was a subaltern in the infantry) and mostly ate our meals together, which were frugal but well spiced with the exuberant high spirits of youth; and

* Friedrich von Hagedorn (1708–54), a minor lyric poet of the so-called 'Anacreontic' school.

† Albrecht von Haller (1708–77), a Swiss, Professor of Medicine at Göttingen. His lyric poetry is didactic in tone and frequently pessimistic in theme, but in *The Alps* a greater sensibility and awareness of nature can be felt.

we were able to prepare them ourselves, for a saveloy with potatoes and lettuce was all there was to have. Wine was a scarce commodity, and to this day I can see Schiller's triumph when he was able to surprise us with a few coppers from his literary earnings. Then the world belonged to us. . . . But gradually the meteor in the literary sky began to arouse enthusiasm. I recollect that several travelling *beaux esprits* in fine coaches halted before our quarters. However flattering such a clientèle may have been, nevertheless for the moment it was not very edifying, for they found him in a state of complete and anything but elegant disarray, in a hole reeking of tobacco, in which, apart from a large table, two benches and a narrow wardrobe hanging on the wall, there was nothing to be found except a great stack of copies of *Die Räuber* in one corner, and in the other a pile of potatoes with empty plates, bottles and the like all in a jumble. A timid and silent perusal of these objects always preceded a conversation.'

This young soldier's sober appraisal recognized something essential when he pointed out the 'stoic stamp' of Schiller's temperament and opinions, and said of him that he would inevitably have become, if not a great poet, then a great figure in public life: 'but it could very easily have been his lot, unhappy but assuredly honourable, to end up in fortress arrest'.

Many tales have been told of his womanizing, but Scharffenstein speaks about his 'lack of sensuality' and says that Schiller did not know quite what to make of women. By that he certainly means the boyishness and impetuous inexperience in Schiller's nature which is so evident in his love-lyrics of this Stuttgart period for all their violent and forceful expressions, and which ever afterwards remain a slightly comic and yet at the same time touching characteristic of Schiller as a love-poet. Admittedly, he frequented the 'soldier's women', as did the others, and afterwards sang his 'manly dignity' in a boastful poem: 'I am a man! who more so than I? whoever can say this, let him prance around freely beneath God's sun and leap up high and sing!'; but to his intimate companion he confessed that the stupidest

D

49

woman is more inscrutable to the most sagacious man than the most obdurate villain. He saw the fruit and plucked it. But his was a heroic soul, too chaste for lingering enjoyment or (still worse) for obscenities.

His landlady in Stuttgart was Luise Vischer, a captain's widow, who was thirty years old at the time. She was no beauty, but had feminine charm and played the piano, which gave much pleasure to her young lodger. It is possible that she never knew that he elevated her to his 'Laura' and wrote the fieriest of love-poems to her. A few years after Schiller had left she again let her room to a pupil from the *Karlsschule*, and with this one she ran away; obviously he did not have the excessive poetic modesty to sit listening while she played the piano, and to write verses to her. But if things were different between Schiller and her in actual fact, and if she did really become an emissary to reconcile him with the world of women, then she performed her task in no unworthy fashion, for it is, after all, no small thing that he should be able to end his hymn of homage *Laura am Klavier* (*Laura at the piano*) with the words:

> Neuer Geister Sonnensitze
> Winken durch zerrissener Himmel Ritze –
> Überm Grabe Morgenrot!
> Weg, ihr Spötter mit Insektenwitze!
> Weg! Es ist ein Gott.*

Incidentally, his mind was much taken up that summer with quite other things than protestations of love. In Mannheim they were waiting for the stage-adaptation of *Die Räuber*, and there was a most inopportune outbreak of dysentery in the Augé regiment. Schiller managed to perform his sick-duty and his poetic labours at the same time, and at last, at the beginning of October, *Die Räuber* was ready for the theatre. He wrote to Dalberg that it would have cost him less effort and given him

---

* 'The radiant thrones of new spirits beckon through the gashes in the skies – dawn rises over the grave! Away, you mockers with the minds of insects! Away! It is a god.'

more pleasure to write a new play than this work. He sent it to Mannheim.

Certain relaxations had been granted recently to Schubart, who was a prisoner in Asperg castle, and in particular he had been granted permission to receive visitors. So now, in November 1781, Schiller, having rid himself of his urgent work, travelled to see him in the company of his fellow-pupil Hoven. Schubart had already read *Die Räuber* and naturally recognized the splendid harvest that had grown out of the seed he himself had sown. They wished to surprise him, and did not tell him at once who stood before him. When he was told, the wretched, ailing man embraced his visitor with tears of joy.

Scarcely had he returned to Stuttgart than Schiller had to learn that even genius may not have too easy a time with the stage. Dalberg made new demands: everything was still too glaring, too strong for him. There were no longer such things as robber bands in their civilized age (as a matter of fact, Swabia had only recently suffered from a few); the play was ticklish, and they would have to transplant it from the present to the age of chivalry if they were to make it manageable for the stage. Schiller tried to defend himself. 'My characters,' he wrote, 'speak in too modern and enlightened a manner for those days. The dialogue is by no means the same. The simplicity which has been so vividly drawn for us by the author of *Goetz von Berlichingen* is totally lacking. Many tirades and traits large and small, characters even, have been lifted straight out of our present-day world and would be of no value at all in the age of Maximilian.'* He complained that they were turning his work into a 'crow with peacock's feathers'. But he added resignedly: 'It is only words, and in fact any theatre can do what it likes with the plays, the author just has to put up with it.'

However, when, on January 13, 1782, the Mannheim performance took place – Schiller had travelled there in secret and without permission from his regiment in the company of Petersen, was admitted to his box a few moments before the curtain

* i.e. Maximilian I, German Emperor 1493–1519.

went up, and sensed the crammed, expectant crowd in the already darkened auditorium – then, for the first time, was revealed the irresistible power over an audience which is this playwright's unique gift, innate, never-failing, triumphing over all obstacles, adaptations and attenuations. People who had read the play or heard it talked about came from the Palatinate, from Worms and Darmstadt, and even from Frankfurt to see it. Many had been unable to obtain tickets. During the early acts the audience waited in silence to see what would happen. The fourth act is set in the gallery of the Moors' castle: Franz Moor and the servant. Now the gap is bridged: it is the moment when the work becomes a unity in both spectator and performer, when it is no longer simply represented up there on the boards, but takes place within all who are present; and that is the moment which decides its success or failure. The superb performance of Iffland,* who was twenty-three at the time, as Franz Moor, undoubtedly made a major contribution. And yet the victory was Schiller's own. For it is surely a part of the genius of a great dramatist that his dramatic vision should also find its proper hour and the intermediaries capable of making it a reality. The stage, like the world itself, is a woman, with whom conquests are only valid if they are not merely dreamed of, but also accomplished. There is a report which describes what went on that evening in the Mannheim theatre: 'Rolling eyes, clenched fists, strangers falling sobbing into one another's arms. . . . Everything dissolved as in the chaos from whose mists a new world breaks forth.'

From the very beginning, the effect produced by Schiller was a revolutionary one. But it must be clearly recognized from the outset that this dramatic insurrection was not directed against any definite set of social conditions. For the worlds of the adversaries in Schiller's plays – Absolutism, the Inquisition, the taskmaster with the feathered hat – disappeared long ago,

---

* August Wilhelm Iffland (1759–1814), a gifted actor, manager and producer who was also the author of a series of sentimental dramas which were very popular in their day.

and yet their effect persists. That is only possible because it is man's immortal soul which here rises up in revolt against restrictions which will not yield up their meaning to it. And because that, of course, is the revolt which concerns us all, and which will never reach its goal as long as the world lasts. 'Aspiring effort', 'achieving essentiality' – these are only labels which at various times have variously been applied to it. Even the false theory of progress still derived its motive power from this source. But the meaning is better revealed – and this is the meaning implied by Schiller's drama – by the old saying that man is a wanderer.

Schiller was honourably received and fêted by Dalberg, by Schwan the bookseller and by the actors; one can imagine that he found it hard to return to his duties as a military surgeon at Stuttgart. The theatre had been revealed to him as the world where the most dazzling fame was to be won, and his experience of the performance had lent wings to all his poetic projects. His letter of thanks to Dalberg emphasizes how much he had learnt in Mannheim about the art of drama. What he is thinking of here is his new play *Die Verschwörung des Fiesko zu Genua* (*The Conspiracy of Fiesko at Genoa*). It was to contain none of the blemishes, he said to Abel, which he himself detected in *Die Räuber*; his reputation as a dramatist would be founded upon his new play. And in fact it does show remarkable progress in the difficult art of dramatic composition, by means of which a complicated plot is comprehended in a series of events which can be viewed as a whole and will thus compel the interest of the spectator. Schiller later achieved a degree of supreme and unsurpassed mastery in this. In *Die Räuber* the author is still led on by the action – he seems to be watching how it unfolds. In the very earliest scenes of *Fiesko*,* which unroll swiftly, powerfully and colourfully, we are confronted with a closely-woven pattern containing all the threads necessary to the action: Fiesko dallies with Julia, the tyrant's sister, and appears to neglect his wife as well as the freedom and honour of the Genoese Republic;

* See synopsis, p. 198-9.

the conspirators (Verrina and Bourgognino), who have fine thoughts of liberty but no ideas on how to overthrow the power of the rulers of Genoa, the Dorias; in the other camp, the Dorias themselves, with the warlike and venerable old Andreas in the background and his loutish nephew, Gianettino, in the foreground; and finally the Moor, as brilliant a rôle as ever a playwright invented, for he is the *grazioso* of the Spanish comedy transplanted to a tragedy in the form of a cut-throat and rascal. With this well-balanced ensemble of instruments the concert is ready to begin. Fiesko, with his superior qualities of leadership, must inevitably be tempted, the victory over tyranny having been won, to make himself a tyrant, and thus fall a victim to the republican wrath of his friend Verrina. A drama of freedom betrayed. Its weakness lies, of course, in the unyieldingness of the man of liberty, Verrina. It may be that we are unable to deduce from his virtuous tirades in the old Roman manner just what sort of a State he wishes to build, but for all that – as so often in Schiller – the *gesture* conveyed by this figure has sufficient conviction to make us recognize him, when he pushes the purple-clad Fiesko from the slippery gangway into the water, as a man acting at the behest of fate. What a tableau! The galley, which the man in purple is about to board, must be a dark shape lying alongside the jetty, a shadowy symbol as if it were the ship of state itself.

An action of state must be 'spun out of the human heart', according to the later preface to the printed edition of this drama. And a lyric poem, too, must become a deed, a sort of raid, even, like that of a bird of prey on a poultry-yard. A Stuttgart poet, Stäudlin, had mockingly called Schiller's poetry 'Siberian', and now produced a *Swabian Muses' Almanac for 1782*, full of a gentle complacency which angered the author of *Die Räuber*. Accordingly, he published his own *Anthology for 1782*, dedicated to 'My master, Death'; the place of publication is given as Tobolsko in Siberia, and the contents proclaim very clearly that the days of cosily sentimental local poetry are numbered. Schiller's friends (Hoven, Haug, Petersen) contributed to the collection, but the great majority of the pieces, which are signed only with initials, are his own work. The odes to 'Laura' were here published for the first time, yet it is not in the love-poem, but in productions like *Die Schlacht* (*The Battle*), *Die Größe der Welt* (*The World's Greatness*), *Gruppe aus dem Tartarus* (*A Group from Tartarus*) and *Der Flüchtling* (*The Fugitive*) that he achieved an early mastery and his own unmistakable note:

> . . . Die Wagen erknarren
> Ins ächzende Tal.
> Die Waldungen leben
> Und Adler und Falken und Habichte schweben
> Und wiegen die Flügel im blendenden Strahl.*

There we have Schiller setting off on an early-morning excursion into his own typical world.

The sequence of events which led to Schiller's flight from his native Swabia can be quickly told. The growing consciousness of his poetic task must in like measure have made Stuttgart, medicine and the army an increasing burden to him. In May he again travelled to Mannheim and seems to have received definite assurances of employment from Dalberg. On this journey, which, like the first, was undertaken secretly and without leave, he had agreeable feminine company: Luise Vischer, the land-lady he had celebrated in verse, and Henriette, the widow of von Wolzogen, a Privy Councillor of Legation, a sincere and pleasant person. She was educating four sons at the *Karlsschule* – Schiller was a life-long friend of Wilhelm – and in addition she had a very pretty daughter, Lotte. Frau von Wolzogen and Frau Vischer wanted to see *Die Räuber* performed in Mannheim. They must subsequently have gossiped about the secret journey, for the affair was reported in minute detail to the Duke. He sent for Schiller. The latter admitted having been in Mannheim, but denied, despite Karl Eugen's threats, the complicity of his

---

* 'The carts creak into the groaning valley. The woodlands come to life, and eagles, falcons and hawks hover on rocking wings in the blinding ray.'

colonel. Schiller was given fourteen days' detention. The conflict with the Duke was aggravated by a ridiculous incident: a
passage in *Die Räuber* where Spiegelberg calls Graubünden 'the
home of rogues' had given offence in that Swiss canton and led
to a protest in the press. Representations were made to the
Duke, and Schiller found himself the occasion of unpleasant-
nesses in international politics. 'I order you, on pain of dismissal, to write no more plays!' he shouted at the poet, if
Petersen's report is true; an express command 'to produce no
more literary work and not to communicate with foreigners'*
was issued – and that really decided the whole affair. One needs
a special insight into the mind of an absolute ruler in order to
understand how he could still lay claim to sentiments of gratitude and attachment from a subject he had treated in this way.
Schiller had sent pleas for help to Dalberg, suggesting how best
he could write to the Duke in order to persuade him to release
Schiller and view the latter's appointment to the Mannheim
theatre as an honour for Württemberg. But Dalberg made no
move. Schiller made similar representations to the Duke (on
September 1, 1782) and requested a relaxation of the ban. The
request was refused, and an order was given to General Augé
that, if he should again report for permission to submit a letter
to His Grace the Duke, he was to be arrested at once.

It thus became necessary to flee. Frau von Wolzogen,
probably frightened by the results of her thoughtless gossip,
promised to receive the poet at Bauerbach, her property in the
Meiningen district, should he ever have need of refuge. It was
courageous of her, for she was, after all, dependent on the Duke
of Württemberg to a certain extent on account of her sons.
Young Andreas Streicher, who wished to go to Hamburg for
training, decided to accompany Schiller. A favourable opportunity to escape was the visit of the Duke's Russian relations,
the Grand Duke (and later Czar) Paul of Russia, which was to
be celebrated with great and extremely expensive festivities.
Both court and city would be on the go. A stag-hunt was

* i.e. subjects of other States.

planned for September 22, and The Solitude was to be illuminated that night.

Among the foreign guests invited to the feast was Dalberg himself, who spoke politely to his playwright but made no firm promises, and the wife of Meyer, the Mannheim producer. She was taken into their confidence, and together with Streicher she accompanied Schiller on a farewell visit to The Solitude, where she found Schiller's mother and Christophine alone. The family had no fear of the Duke's revenge; for all the ease and matter-of-course arrogance with which they exercised their tyranny, there were still things which it was thought unsuitable for the rulers of those days to do. But they nevertheless kept from the father his son's plan to flee, in order to make it possible for him, when interrogated, to answer on his word of honour that he had known nothing of it. When he came into the room and began to speak about the preparations for the festival, Schiller left unnoticed with his mother, and returned alone; she could not let them see her tearful face.

Schiller's belongings had been carefully taken to Streicher's rooms, since a vehicle could drive up there and the belongings be loaded into it with less chance of attracting attention. At ten o'clock on the last morning the rest of Schiller's luggage was to be ready to be fetched from his quarters. Streicher has related how he turned up punctually – but nothing was ready: 'For after Schiller had returned at 8 a.m. from his last visit to the hospital, whilst packing his books the Odes of Klopstock came into his hand, and one of them, which had always attracted him, now excited him so much that he at once – and at such a decisive moment! – composed a companion-piece.' It was in vain that Streicher urged haste; he had to hear the ode, and then the companion-piece. It was a long time before he managed to bring the poet back 'to the present day and the fleeting minute'.

That evening, after the vehicle had been loaded with two trunks and a small piano, Streicher, himself an only son, also took a heavy farewell of his mother, and they set off. They went out by the Esslingen gate, where they were hailed: 'Halt!

who goes there? What are the gentlemen's names?' Streicher replied for both of them: 'Dr Ritter and Dr Wolf, travelling to Esslingen.' They were through. Then they had to circle the town in order to reach the road to Ludwigsburg. To the left of Ludwigsburg they saw a glow in the sky, and then, upon its eminence, the castle of The Solitude, sparkling with a thousand lights in festive splendour. The air was so clear and everything so distinct in the brightness that Schiller was able from the distance to point out to his friend the house where his parents dwelt. And then it struck the fugitive what he was leaving behind, his family and his home; and the other heard him say softly: 'My mother.'

CHAPTER IV

MANNHEIM AND BAUERBACH
(September 1782-July 1783)

*

The first person Schiller visited in Mannheim was Meyer. Meyer was Dalberg's chief producer, as we would say today, and the running of the theatre during the manager's absence was in his hands. He had respect and genuine sympathy for Schiller, but he was frightened now that Schiller was standing before him as a destitute fugitive who hoped for support from Dalberg: he may have known all too well how frail such a hope was.

He did not let his fright appear too noticeable; he invited Schiller and Streicher to dinner and found them lodgings near his own house, but urged the poet to seek a reconciliation with his monarch. After dinner Schiller sat down at Meyer's writing-table and composed a letter in which Karl Eugen was addressed as 'Prince and father'. Schiller explained to him that he had only left his home because he had been threatened with arrest as soon as he submitted his petition for the lifting of the ban on literary activity. 'I await your most gracious answer trembling with hope, impatient to hurry home from a strange country to my Prince and my Fatherland. Languishing in deepest submission, and with all the feelings of a son towards his wrathful father, I am Your Serene Highness's most submissive, loyal and obedient servant Schiller.'

This letter cannot be taken at its face value. It was obviously intended to prevent Schiller's flight from being interpreted as open rebellion which might yet be avenged on his family. For when General Augé, to whom Schiller had sent both his petition and a request for mediation with the Duke, sent two replies, the second of which was even more favourable than the first, so that Schiller could well have expected an indulgent reception had he returned to Württemberg, he still did not consent to do so, although his experiences in Mannheim must certainly have urged such a course upon him. He knew that, even though he might be treated with a greater or lesser degree of friendliness, he would still have ceased to be a free man. And one may trust Schiller to be aware of the ridiculousness of first gaining a taste of freedom and then creeping back to his collar and chain. But as if that were not enough, we have the letter written that same autumn to a friend in Stuttgart, Jacobi. It may be true that, in the messages sent to Swabia, he expressed greater confidence than he really felt, and also that he sprinkled them with a number of deliberately misleading remarks in order to divert the persecution he feared – but here, in the letter to Jacobi, it is patent that he desires not to be misunderstood by a person with whom he has close ties. It must be taken as an expression of his true state of mind when he writes: 'I should have thought you would have judged me, not by my letters, but by my actions, which are the precise opposite of the former.'

He paid dearly for his resolve to hold out at all costs in his state of freedom. Hercules of the twelve labours was no favourite of fortune: the gods did not spare him the severest tests.

First of all, Frau Meyer, who returned from Stuttgart, had all sorts of things to tell of the excitement which his flight had caused there; everyone expected that the Duke would proceed violently against Schiller, as in the case of Schubart a few years before. Schiller would do better, the Meyers both thought, not to show himself in Mannheim. But they invited a circle of friends to their rooms, to whom Schiller was to read aloud his new work, *Fiesko*, which was almost completed. This painful and comic episode, which Streicher describes at length, is so typical of the perennially difficult relationship between poetry and the stage that it is worth recording here. Streicher describes how they all arrived: Iffland, Beil, Beck and several other actors; how they expressed to the poet their respect and their high expectations of his new work. They sat down together at a large round table, and Schiller began to read.

But the first act, and then the second, were listened to attentively but without any applause. Then they got up, because refreshments were being served. One actor (Streicher could have murdered him for it) proposed a shooting-contest. 'But after a quarter of an hour they had all drifted away; apart from those who lived in the house, only Iffland remained, and he did not leave till eight at night. Streicher, indignant, wanted to complain to their host about the scornful way the poet had been treated. Meyer took him into the next room and asked: 'Tell me honestly, are you sure that it was Schiller who wrote *Die Räuber*?'

Streicher: 'Absolutely! How can you doubt it?'

Meyer: 'Because *Fiesko* is the worst thing I have ever heard in my life, and because it is impossible that the same Schiller who wrote *Die Räuber* could have produced such a wretched, common-place piece of work.' And when Streicher insisted, he concluded: 'If Schiller really wrote *Die Räuber* and *Fiesko*, then he exhausted his powers in the first piece and now can produce nothing but miserable, bombastic, meaningless rubbish.'

The evening passed in deadly embarrassment, and not another word was spoken about *Fiesko*. Schiller was very upset and left early, but Meyer still had the politeness to ask to keep the manuscript overnight, in order to find out how the play ended. Depressed, the two friends strolled back to their lodgings, in silence at first, but then Schiller exploded and complained about the actors' lack of understanding. But if he didn't succeed here as a playwright, then he would appear as an actor. 'For really,' he said, 'no one can declaim as well as I can.'

Early the next morning, in a state of nervous expectancy, Streicher went to Meyer to hear his final verdict on *Fiesko* – only to hear the latter call out to him: 'You are right! *Fiesko* is a masterpiece and much better done than *Die Räuber*. But do you know why we all thought it the most awful rubbish? It was Schiller's Swabian accent and his confounded habit of declaiming everything. He recites everything in the same bombastic tones, whether it is just "He closes the door" or an important passage. But now the play must come before the committee ... we will move heaven and earth to get it performed as soon as we can.'

Dalberg had not yet returned from Stuttgart, and the Meyers did not think the poet was safe in Mannheim. It was decided that, for the time being, he should go with Streicher to Frankfurt am Main, from where Streicher could continue on his way to Hamburg. The two friends' ready cash was running low, and they had to travel on foot. The excitements and decisions of recent days had had their effect on Schiller, and the two days' journey tired him greatly. Partly for reasons of economy, and partly to be safer from inquiry, they took lodgings, not in Frankfurt itself, but in the suburb of Sachsenhausen near the Main bridge; and from here Schiller wrote to Dalberg. It is easy to recognize how hard it was for him to write the letter, but he describes his desperate situation to him without concealment, and confesses himself 'destitute of money and hope. I could blush for shame at having to make such admissions to you, but I know that I am not demeaning myself.' He is concerned above all to pay his debts in Stuttgart in order to rescue a friend from danger who, himself penniless, has stood surety for him there. For himself he requests a 'kind advance' on the new play, some payment which will support him for the time being.

A portrait of this Heribert Dalberg reveals something smug and self-satisfied about him, and a bad forehead which betrays his lack of a sense of intellectual responsibility. Nobody could expect such a man-about-the-court to take the part of the fugitive poet, who had been incited to this course in no small degree by his own assurances, and to expose himself to unpleasantness with a neighbouring ruler. One finds it, if not exactly admirable, then at least understandable that he held back and avoided a meeting. But to perform an author who was already known throughout Germany was neither a political nor an artistic risk; the sum requested was trifling, and could easily be recouped by the Genoese play. But Dalberg, as if he had not just received a declaration of the most pressing need, sent neither an advance nor an acceptance; instead, he demanded through Meyer a reshaping of the play, which he then, after it had been carried out through several laborious weeks, rejected as unsuitable. In consequence, he said, the play could not be accepted, and no payment could be made on it.

We can read in Streicher's account how Schiller received the first of these pieces of bad news: 'Not a single hard or violent word crossed his lips, in fact he did not even deign to criticize the reply he had received. . . . His only thought was what was to be done first of all.' But Karoline von Wolzogen recalls that Schiller spoke of 'very gloomy moments' which he endured on the bridge over the Main at Sachsenhausen, and Lotte Schiller said: 'I should like to raise a memorial to him there.' We know no more about the dark shadow that passed over him just then.

At the same time as the disappointment he experienced with Dalberg, he received from Andreas Streicher a sacrifice of friendship which was all the finer for being made in such a quiet and matter-of-course way. Streicher made his mother send him the money it had taken him years to save, and which he had earmarked for his music studies in Hamburg. He gave it as his reason that he could not leave Schiller in the lurch now. His diaries of Schiller's needy years in Mannheim, wherever one opens them, reveal him clearly to us as a man without falsehood or self-seeking, one of those rare beings in whom the rather faded notion of loyalty once more achieves life and distinctness.

It has been related that Streicher brought a small piano with him. As the Meyers had in the meantime discovered a modest inn in Oggersheim near Mannheim where Schiller (under the new pseudonym of 'Dr Schmidt') was to live undisturbed and complete the adaptation of *Fiesko*, they transferred their combined luggage out there – it was about the middle of October

– and in the weeks of hard work that followed Streicher brightened his friend's evenings with his piano playing. Schiller 'usually asked as early as midday, with the most confiding modesty, "Will you not play the piano again this evening?" When dusk fell his wish was fulfilled, during which time he paced the room, which was often lit only by the moon, for several hours, and not infrequently broke out into indistinct cries of enthusiasm.'

During the darkest hours in Sachsenhausen the outline of a new dramatic work revealed itself with unexpected clarity to Schiller. It was *Luise Miller*, which later, through Iffland, came to be called *Kabale und Liebe* (*Love and Intrigue*). It is possible, as another tradition relates, that the first sketch goes back to the fourteen days' arrest in Stuttgart. This was the play which engrossed all his faculties in Oggersheim, so that he had to write down the plan and begin the actual composition, and only with an effort could he force himself back to *Fiesko*. In November – *Fiesko* had been delivered to Dalberg, whose answer was still awaited – a Württemberg officer appeared at the Meyers' house in Mannheim and asked after Schiller. He was a comrade from the *Karlsschule* and wanted to see him again. But that only emerged subsequently. The man in uniform was thought to have been commissioned by Karl Eugen to arrest the poet, and they agreed that Schiller could not remain in the Mannheim neighbourhood, but must avail himself of Frau von Wolzogen's offer of refuge in Bauerbach. He wished, before travelling so far away, to see his own people once more. A meeting was arranged for November 22 in Bretten. His mother and Christophine travelled there and sat waiting anxiously in the darkened inn; they heard hoofbeats and recognized the rider's voice when, in the next room, he asked the waiter for them. Schiller appeared in good spirits and full of optimism, and chatted till morning. They enjoyed three days there together. More than ten years were to pass before they saw each other again.

After Dalberg's refusal, *Fiesko* was sold to Schwan, the

bookseller who had already published the stage version of *Die Räuber*. The fee sufficed to pay the innkeeper in Oggersheim, and for the journey to Meiningen. There could be no thought of covering the debts in Stuttgart or of making good Streicher's expenditures; the latter had to give up his plan of studying in Hamburg, and seek a meagre living in Mannheim. Without an overcoat (he was too poor to buy one) and with only a light top-coat, Schiller now travelled for seven days in a mailcoach from Worms to Meiningen, a cold, wearisome journey, for winter had now set in, and with it notably low temperatures. On December 7, a Saturday, in the Stag at Meiningen, he met Wilhelm Friedrich Reinwald, a librarian; the meeting had been arranged by Frau von Wolzogen. The poet, whose heart was always open to friendship, developed a lively attachment to this cultured, good-natured man, who was a bachelor and something of an eccentric; during the months of rustic solitude in Bauerbach that followed, Reinwald was his only source of intellectual companionship. Schiller was a man who needed people, not in order to consume them or take exclusive possession of them, but because he was of a sociable disposition. 'Thoughts,' he wrote, 'can only be enticed out by thoughts, and our mental powers, like the strings of an instrument, need fiddlers to play them.' Some years later Reinwald married Christophine Schiller, against the wishes of her brother, who attempted to talk her out of it on account of his hypochondria and unfittedness for marriage. But when the union did nevertheless take place, he demanded that his dissuading letters should be laid before his friend, so that all could remain clear and above board in a relationship which otherwise might easily go awry: a direct way of going about things which is characteristic of him.

On that same Saturday evening in December he travelled on to Bauerbach. He did not stay in the actual manor, which was not fit for living in at the time, but in the village itself in a cottage belonging to the lady of the manor. The village lies two hours south of Meiningen on the high ground between the

Werra and the Main. A watercourse runs through the lonely valley between willows and adlers. He had peace and protection there, and one can sense his holiday mood in the letter he wrote on the very next day, December 8, to Streicher: 'I am here at last, happy and contented to have gained the shore. I found that everything surpasses my expectations. . . . I am no longer troubled by urgent needs, and no outside interference shall disturb my poetic dreams. Frau von Wolzogen's house is a very pretty place, and I do not miss the town at all. I have every comfort – food, service, linen, heating and the like are all most fully and willingly provided by the people of the village. I arrived here in the evening . . . showed my letters of introduction and was at once conducted ceremoniously to the house where they had already cleaned everything, lit the fires and procured beds.' He intended 'to do a fearful amount of work' here, the letter to Streicher continues, 'the Easter Fair had better look out for itself' . . . and then comes a note of bitter recollection of what he had suffered in Mannheim: 'Whatever you do, do not lose sight of the following practical truth, which I have purchased all too dearly: if one has need of human beings, one has either to be a cur, or else makes oneself indispensable to them; either the one or the other, else one will perish.' In a letter to Schwan of the same date he begs him to take care of Streicher, 'support him with advice and recommendations. It will be as if you were doing it to *me*'.

So there, in his rustic cottage, Schiller sat and wrote in a tiny, low-ceilinged room by the big tiled stove. He was in the warm, but lonelier than ever, for a man who had grown up in a barracks, which is what the *Karlsschule* really was, was unfamiliar with the total isolation he now experienced in Bauerbach, when all the roads were snowed up so as to be almost impassable. He felt as if he had been forgotten by the world, but he did not himself forget it. Scarcely ten days had passed before he said in a letter to Reinwald that he longed to see human faces, that he wanted to meet Reinwald, and that he must know what the theatrical journal said about *Die Räuber*;

and his new tragedy (i.e. *Luise Miller*) would soon be finished.

This tragedy,* of course, was not of a kind that could be written in a mood of renunciation, for in it Schiller, with the immediacy of his own experience, contends with that absolutism which reduces men either to rogues or to servile toadies; which gives a ruler the opportunity of selling his subjects abroad so that he may adorn his mistress's hair with diamonds; and which dares to reject the word of frank assent uttered when heart encounters heart, because it views a difference of social status as an unbridgeable gap. The drama remains on the revolutionary plane which, as we have already seen in *Die Räuber*, points forward to the realm of the metaphysical, without yet attaining to the sublime level on which ultimate things are divined and interpreted, as in *Don Carlos* and *Wallenstein*. But on its own level this play about middle-class love and court intrigue represents mastery already attained, and even in the play in which he reached the summit of classical composition, *Maria Stuart* – which, incidentally, he was already thinking and scheming over during the Bauerbach period – Schiller was unable to produce a neater and clearer piece of work than in *Luise Miller*. He conveys everything that the play seeks to say through action, not ratiocination – or perhaps it should be more correctly expressed as follows: his ratiocination does not impede his action, but is its driving force. The course of the action has that admirable sureness, never deviating, never even hesitating, which Schiller could only have learnt, alone among German models, from Lessing's *Emilia Galotti*. The texture is not as transparent and fine as in Lessing, but it is just as firm; once the listener has been caught in it, it does not for a minute let him go. The characters are like knots in the net stretched round the lovers, Ferdinand and Luise: President Walter, with his ambition for a mock-marriage between his son and Lady Milford which will reinforce his influence; Secretary Wurm, an ugly man with designs on the musician's pretty daughter; on

* Renamed *Kabale und Liebe* for its first performance and ever since. See synopsis, p. 199.

the other side, Luise's father and mother; the internal links: the Chamberlain, the valet, the lady's maid Sophie. There is nothing that does not contribute to the total effect, an achievement which has survived changing times, transcending the limitations and the historical context of its subject. And yet these characters, like all those in Schiller, speak, even in the most passionate argument, an intellectually heightened language, even the middle-class girl to the Lady, like card players staking and then trumping: 'Forgive me, madam. I was on the point of weeping over this gorgeous, flashing ruby, which must not know that its owner is so enraged against vanity.' *These* people, the ones the author wishes to present here, ought not to talk like this; the effect *should* be unconvincing, even ridiculous; but it achieves conviction through the transporting mime of this tragic puppet-play worked by Schiller's fingers, which in the theatre – as every performance demonstrates – no one can resist.

Schiller's impatient mind ranged beyond the work he had in hand to still further plans. *Luise Miller* had not been finished, but his thoughts were already turning towards a *Don Carlos*. Reinwald had provided him with the necessary books from the Meiningen library. Out of the sad historical facts concerning the physically and mentally deficient Carlos, Infante of Spain, whom the Queen took pity on and cared for, the inventive Abbé Saint-Real had constructed an interesting little French court tale. We know that Schiller got his material from this dubious authority, but what he made of it was a palace built on the ground-plan of a salon. He wrote to Reinwald: 'I will make it my duty in this play to avenge prostituted humanity in depicting the Inquisition, and to pillory most fearfully the blots on its history. I wish to thrust deep into the heart of a type of man which the dagger of tragedy has so far only grazed.'

The author of these gloomy schemes was twenty-three years old. Out of fear of possible pursuit and out of consideration for his hostess he still concealed his name; to the inhabitants of Bauerbach he was the mysterious stranger who sat over his books, smoking his pipe, always immersed in work. But when his patroness, Frau von Wolzogen, came from Stuttgart for a short visit with her sixteen-year-old daughter Lotte, he livened up and set the whole village preparing a festive welcome for their revered and beloved mistress. He made them erect an avenue of shrubbery, a gate of honour was constructed from fir-branches, and to the accompaniment of a salute of cannonry they proceeded to church, where the pastor preached a sermon of welcome. There now followed a feverish period, short but intense, during which Schiller was infatuated with Lotte von Wolzogen, to whom he had already been attracted in Stuttgart. Luise Miller acquired shape and colour from the figure of this lively young creature, and in real life as in the play a difference in social station was involved: the noblewoman was forbidden to the middle-class Schiller. But the Wolzogen girl obviously escaped the tragic experience which her poet underwent; she seems never to have looked on him with eyes of love, for her affections were engaged elsewhere, and later she married a government official of noble birth and found happiness with him.

But even Schiller's love for this first Lotte to cross his path was really no more than a green woodland dream, an infatuation almost without an object, generated by his own youthful, lonely, unoccupied feelings, which afterwards, when Henriette von Wolzogen returned to Bauerbach without her daughter, attached themselves to her with a tenderness of which he was oblivious. For she was alone, had suffered many disappointments, and at forty was not so old as to be stranger to all desire; perhaps she would have liked to keep the poet with her, even though she must have been well aware that it was impossible. Schiller's letters subsequent to the Bauerbach period make it clear that such indeterminate feelings did exist, but they also show that none of it ever came to words.

Kaspar Schiller had written to beg Schwan, the Mannheim bookseller, to advise his son's return to medicine, which the father saw as his only sensible livelihood. And medicine was continually spoken of in the poet's plans, too; his debts worried him, and the practice of medicine would provide an assured income and with it the possibility of settling them. But it was his literary projects which filled his heart and mind. And then when Dalberg unexpectedly expressed his interest in Schiller's new drama and wished once more to call him to Mannheim, the poet compelled himself to compose an answer in terms of calm politeness, whereas in fact his decision had already been made. Frau von Wolzogen exacted a promise from him that he would seek adequate guarantees in his negotiations with Dalberg, and above all that he would not offer himself, which could only lower his value in the eyes of such a man of affairs. But she was wise enough to know that great men cannot be sheltered from their deeds and sufferings. She saw, too, that the parting was not, as he honestly believed, for a few weeks. He went, and the times that had been would not return. She helped him with money and gifts as a mother would her son, even though she could only lend him the money, for her own circumstances were by no means opulent. In July, 1783, he left the forest vale of Bauerbach and travelled out into the world again.

CHAPTER V

MANNHEIM—A THEATRE CONTRACT
(1783-85)

*

The most difficult and disappointing period of Schiller's years of travel now began. In Mannheim he was received with all the old cordiality by the Meyers and particularly by the faithful Streicher. But the head of the Mannheim theatre was away, and since all future arrangements depended upon a conversation with him, Schiller was obliged to waste a fortnight in the town, sweltering in the summer heat and watching his meagre purse dwindling daily. Dalberg, as soon as he returned, received the poet 'in the most courteous manner and with the greatest respect', and soon induced him to conclude a year's contract, under which Schiller was appointed resident playwright and was engaged at a fee of 300 Imperial Florins to deliver three plays – those meant were *Fiesko* in a new version, *Luise Miller* and *Don Carlos*. Since Duke Karl Eugen seemed to have decided to show that he, too, could be as tolerant as the great Frederick and would pursue Schiller no longer, Mannheim no longer risked any unpleasantness by engaging him, and anyway the young man was enjoying an astounding and ever-growing fame. That same winter he was admitted by a free vote to the 'German Society' of Mannheim, a picked band of leading authors and men of learning. For an ambitious theatre-manager he was really a valuable acquisition. Schiller, too, was happy: 'His satisfaction at the appointment,' relates Streicher, 'could be seen in every word and every glance.' He knew that he was born for the theatre and now saw himself firmly bound to a leading stage; he also took part in the sittings of the Theatre

Committee. He was in his element. In a letter to Frau von Wolzogen he nevertheless expresses the opinion that he would never have committed himself in Mannheim if she had not written to him that the young Herr von Winckelmann was coming on a visit to Bauerbach. The latter was Schiller's rival for the hand of young Lotte. He did not wish to see him, and declared him to be the real reason for his staying away. And even in the summer of the following year, in the midst of all the complications in Mannheim, a letter of Schiller's in which he is enthusing about the bliss of quietness suddenly turns into what is almost a written application for her daughter's hand. 'Lotte would never be rich, but she would certainly be happy.' We do not know the nature of her reply, but we can imagine the feeling of mingled amusement and melancholy with which the mother received such confessions.

Scarcely had Schiller signed the theatre contract than he was attacked by an endemic fever which was around in Mannheim and which seriously impaired his capacity for work and his mental mood. The illness was combatted with quinine and fasting. 'I live wretchedly enough,' he complains, 'in order to get rid of [the fever]. For a fortnight I have seen neither meat nor broth. Nothing but gruel day in, day out, and so it goes on morning and night. Perhaps a few carrots or sour potatoes with it. I eat China bark like bread and have had it specially prescribed for me from Frankfurt.' This violent cure by hunger and poison, during which, moreover, he had to work strenuously to produce the stage adaptations of *Fiesko* and *Luise Miller*, seriously affected him; he felt 'that this winter has really gravely affected my constitution, perhaps for life'.

This was the situation in which he was found by Abel, his teacher from the *Karlsschule*, who came to Mannheim to see him in November, accompanied by another professor from Stuttgart, Baz. Schiller was pleased about the visit; he served them burgundy which acquaintances in Mannheim had given him in order to help him gain strength, and conducted his friends round the town, although he should have kept to his room. 'It doesn't matter,' he wrote, 'if it takes me longer to get better; after all, it has given me indescribable pleasure.' And Abel describes how Schiller, after they had discussed his circumstances and uncertain future, 'suddenly walked up to me and full of courage and self-confidence assured me that a time would come when his name would be spoken throughout the length and breadth of Germany'.

On January 11, 1784, *Fiesko* was given its first performance, the play which Dalberg had so off-handedly rejected in the version published by Schwan, as well as in the Oggersheim stage adaptation. The further treatment to which it had been subjected in Mannheim must have been largely to accord with the wishes of the impresario; it was cut down to the length of one evening's performance, reduced in number of characters, moderated in expression in accordance with the audience's ideas of propriety, and, above all, the conclusion was a happy instead of a tragic one. Fiesko is no longer drowned because the power he has gained turns him into a tyrant; instead, he renounces the crown, Verrina falls enthusiastically into his arms, and the people of Genoa are called upon to admire in Fiesko their 'happiest citizen'. Artistically this is most certainly an unsatisfying happy ending imposed from without, since it does not emerge credibly from the character of Fiesko as we have come to know him during the four previous acts. But Dalberg, for all his *savoir faire*, seems not to have noticed that the new ending is even more revolutionary than the first one was. For if a nation rejoicing in the abdication of a prince is 'a heavenly spectacle, more rewarding than all the crowns in the world', then strictly speaking the idea was here expressed which fifteen years later could be read in Hölderlin's *Empedocles*: 'The age of kings is past.'

Fiesko was put on the stage 'with much preparation'; the author himself had conducted the rehearsals. But the public, expecting a picture of Rousseauistic naturalism in the manner of *Die Räuber*, could not make anything of this story of Genoese politics. 'Republican freedom,' as Schiller put it in a letter to

Reinwald, 'is a meaningless noise in this country . . . no Roman blood flows in the veins of the good citizens of the Palatinate.' Probably he did them an injustice, and it was the distorted ending which the listeners could not stomach. In Berlin, in another stage adaptation, *Fiesko* was performed with considerable success, and in Vienna the Emperor Joseph II even made his own version of the work, in which he detected sentiments akin to his own, and had it performed in his *Burgtheater*.*

In Mannheim the lukewarm reception of the Genoese piece was soon made up for by the brilliant acclaim accorded on April 15, 1784, to *Kabale und Liebe* (*Love and Intrigue*) – this was the new title for *Luise Miller* thought up by Iffland on the occasion of the première. In his memoirs Streicher gives an account of the evening, which he spent in the box with Schiller. 'Calm, cheerful, but absorbed in his own thoughts and only exchanging an occasional word, [Schiller] awaited the rustle of the ascending curtain. But then when the action began: the look of intense expectancy, the play of the upper and lower lip, the frown when something was not spoken as he would wish it, the flashing eyes when passages calculated to produce an effect actually did so – who can describe these things? During the whole of the first act not a word escaped his lips, and only at its conclusion was he heard to say: "It's going well." The second act became very lively, and its ending in particular was acted with such fire and gripping truth that, after the curtain had already fallen, all the spectaters rose to their feet in a manner quite unusual at that time and burst, shouting and clapping, into tempestuous and unanimous applause. The author was so surprised by it that he rose to his feet and bowed to the audience. In his mien and his proud, noble bearing was to be seen the consciousness that he had done himself justice.'

Soon afterwards Schiller travelled to Frankfurt am Main

* Literally: 'Castle Theatre', which was founded in 1776 by the Emperor Joseph II as a national home of 'serious' German drama (as opposed to the 'popular' pieces of the ancient Viennese theatre, which were relegated to the suburbs). It remains to this day the premier stage in the German-speaking countries.

with the actors Iffland and Beil, who had to give guest performances there, at the invitation of the Frankfurt theatre-manager Grossmann, who had also produced *Kabale und Liebe*, two days, in fact, before the Mannheim company, and who now put on a special performance in the author's honour. From a letter written by Goethe's mother we learn that the play was a great draw in Frankfurt as well, and Schiller took a youthful pleasure in being fêted as a celebrated guest. While there he made the acquaintance of an actress, Sophie Albrecht, who was married to a doctor. Schiller took a lively interest in her and wanted to talk her out of the life of the theatre, but she was unable to renounce it. She is reported as having had 'an expressive countenance, with an ardent gaze and a passionately attractive nature'. She admired Schiller's poetry and even wrote verses to him. These happy days in Frankfurt were to be his last before his insecurely-based life in Mannheim took a sudden turn for the worse.

At the beginning of May he wrote to Reinwald that it was entirely up to him whether he (Schiller) wished to renew his contract with Dalberg for the coming year. But even then something seems to have been not quite in order. Could it be that Iffland who, after all, was not only an important actor but also the author of unimportant sentimental bourgeois pieces, viewed Schiller as a rival, now that in *Kabale und Liebe* he had poached on his preserve as a purveyor of bourgeois tragedies? Or did it really lie with Dalberg, whose nature, like too soft a soil, could bear low shrubs but no trees? We will never know for sure. For such a tangle of circumstances, interests and intrigues cannot be fully unravelled even by one who was immediately engaged, let alone by the distant observer. What is clearly recognizable from the series of letters sent to Dalberg is Schiller's effort to obtain an extension of the contract, and Dalberg's evasion, which finally led to his even advising Schiller to return to medicine. We observe with amazement how the poet accepted this shameless suggestion with good-natured gratitude as a sign of warm concern for his fate – but we do not know whether to admire it as a piece of genuine, touching guilelessness or as higher diplomacy; for in fact the manner in which Schiller received the proposal was the only way out if he was honourably to avoid an immediate break with Dalberg. The hostility of the old hands of the establishment towards the poet, who did not fit into their world, reached a point during the height of the summer of 1784 at which a play called *Der schwarze Mann* (*The Man in Black*) was put on at Mannheim, in which the author, Gotter, a manufacturer of comedies highly thought of in his day, was allowed to pillory the author of *Die Räuber* and *Fiesko* as 'the playwright Expletive'.* Schiller again could only defend himself against this insult by not appearing to understand it.

There were political machinations as well as theatrical ones. Schiller was anonymously denounced to the Elector of Bavaria in Munich as the author of plays 'which are the occasion of bad examples'. On top of that there was the continual, oppressive lack of money, for Mannheim was expensive, and Schiller, who could put up with many privations, had no talent for cheese-paring. Frau von Wolzogen could have done with the money she had lent him, but he could not afford to send any to her, and tormented himself over it.

Amid such troubles, *Don Carlos*, which, according to the terms of the contract, he had still to deliver during the current year, made but slow progress. 'It is understandable,' writes Andreas Streicher, who observed at close quarters all this misery and the tireless courage of Schiller's struggle, 'that the eye-witness of this situation, the poet's friend, could never bring himself in later days to see a performance of any of these three plays [*Fiesko, Kabale und Liebe, Don Carlos*]. As often as he made the attempt, he was obliged to depart after the very first scene, because he was overcome by such pain and melancholy as could only be calmed in the open air.'

In June 1784 Schiller saw for the first time the girl who was destined to be his wife. Frau von Lengefeld with her daughters

* His German name *Flickwort* (literally: 'Patch-word') is more expressive.

Karoline and Lotte and the fiancé of the elder, a Herr von Beulwitz, passed through Mannheim on their way home from a journey to Switzerland. They wished to meet the famous author of *Die Räuber*. From Stuttgart they had paid a visit to his people at The Solitude, and brought him greetings from them. But Schiller was late in receiving the cards announcing their visit, and only appeared when they were on the point of departure. The meeting therefore only lasted a moment. Yet Karoline and Lotte marvelled afterwards 'that such a powerful, untamed genius should possess such a mild exterior'.

About the same time a letter and packets reached Schiller from Leipzig, in which four unknown people expressed to him their admiration and gratitude for his writings. 'In an age in which art is becoming increasingly the mercenary slave of rich and powerful libertines, it is a relief when a great man steps forward and shows what even now humanity is able to achieve' – thus the communication opened. The tone is Schiller's own – it is an echo of his voice, the language of a young man, heightened by enthusiasm; but this man's feelings were so pure and assured that his words only expressed what in fact was and to this day still is true of the poet. 'To show what humanity is still able to achieve' – that was his mission; it could not be more tersely put. The writer of the letter was called Gottfried Körner, the others were his fiancée and her sister, Minna and Dora Stock, and a friend, Ludwig Ferdinand Huber. With the letter came an embroidered wallet, a setting of a song from *Die Räuber* and drawings of their four young and attractive faces. However, Schiller did not at first learn what their names were – indeed his days in Mannheim were so occupied that it was impossible for him for months on end, right into December, to find the time to acknowledge their gesture.

On June 26 he had to deliver a lecture to the German Society, of which he was a member, and this gave him the opportunity of pronouncing upon his conception of the drama. He called it *What can a good standing theatre actually accomplish?* In his works it appears under the title *Die Schaubühne als moral-*

ische Anstalt (*The Theatre as a Moral Institution*), and was then somewhat prematurely taken to be the theoretical basis and guiding principle of Schiller's dramatic work. Certainly, he first developed here the idea to which as a mature artist he gave such unforgettable form in the ballad *Die Kraniche des Ibykus* (*The Cranes of Ibykus*),* that the action of the drama, by piercing to the heart of the spectator, unmasks the guilty and turns the stage into a tribunal; 'a living flame of desire for virtue, a burning hatred of vice' are aroused by it, he says. And this effect, where achieved, would indeed give a genuine significance to the theatre. But Schiller goes further. Lessing had said that it was a 'desperate notion' to think that the Germans should possess a national theatre without previously becoming a nation, but Schiller had youth, courage and faith enough to turn Lessing's sceptical pronouncement into its converse: 'If ever we lived to see ourselves in possession of a national theatre, we should also be a nation.' And proceeding beyond even this goal, describing the happy moment when the crowd of people assembled in the theatre are united in their experience of what is going on on the stage, he concludes: 'Then finally – what a triumph for thee, Nature, so often trampled to the ground, so often rising again, when men of all circles and regions and classes . . . brothers in one all-embracing sympathy . . . forget themselves and forget the world and draw near to their heavenly origin. Each individual enjoys the ecstasy of all . . . and his breast can find room for one and only one sensation: that of being a *man*.'

It was at that same time that Schiller's financial worries suddenly became very acute and immediate. The principal item in Schiller's Stuttgart debts was the sum he had borrowed three years ago to pay for the first printing of *Die Räuber*. A corporal's wife in Stuttgart had negotiated and gone surety for the loan;

* A ballad on a Classical theme, which tells how Ibykus, the sixth-century Greek poet, is murdered on a journey to Corinth, and in dying calls on a flight of passing cranes to witness to his death. Later, at the Olympic games, the same cranes fly over, causing one of the murderers to cry: 'Look! Ibykus' cranes!' and thus reveal their guilt.

78

she came to Mannheim, fleeing from her creditors, where the latter now, however, had her imprisoned. Neither with Dalberg, Schwan nor any other of his affluent Mannheim acquaintances were Schiller's relations such that he could beg their assistance in an affair of this nature; but in order to obtain the release of the corporal's wife, whose reputation, moreover, was not of the best, hard cash must be forthcoming. At just this time, July 1784, Schiller had his sister Christophine staying with him, and Reinwald had come to Mannheim with her, having first conducted a correspondence with Christophine and afterwards presented himself at The Solitude as her suitor. Presumably the engaged couple, and in particular the staid and respectable Reinwald, were not supposed to know anything about his future brother-in-law's debts and the corporal's wife in gaol, so Schiller had to play the cheerful host, while the water rose right up to his chin. An appeal to his father brought him admonishment, which made bitter reading, but no help. Kaspar Schiller had only a meagre salary and three daughters still unprovided for, and since his son, as soon as cheerful prospects brightened the horizon, had been glad to paint an all-too-rosy picture of his situation, he probably thought now that he had got himself into these serious difficulties through his own frivolity. Rescue came from an unexpectedly close quarter. The master-mason, Hölzel, and his wife, with whom Schiller and Streicher lodged in Mannheim, noticed the poet's troubled state, or perhaps Streicher had dropped hints – so these good people offered their help and provided him with the necessary sum. On his departure from Mannheim Schiller repaid this money. Fifteen years later the French came to Mannheim, and with them the trials of war and occupation; the Hölzel family got into difficulties, and Schiller was able to assist them financially and procure a job for their son as a scene-shifter in the Mannheim theatre.

Apart from Streicher, the Hölzels provided the most touching human experience of Schiller's Mannheim days. But we must attempt to describe the large, animated circle of people who surrounded him there. First of all there was Schwan, the very capable publisher and bookseller, everyone's confidential friend and the intellectual hub of the town, at whose house congregated authors, journalists and actors. When Mannheim was seeking a director for its National Theatre, Lessing was the first man thought of and Schwan was sent to Wolfenbüttel* to see him. Schwan also had connections with Wieland,† and of course Schiller himself had been put in touch by him with Dalberg. His wife was no longer living, and his nineteen-year-old daughter Margarethe, a beautiful, dark-eyed, lively-minded girl, kept house for him. She made Schiller read her anything new he had written, while the younger daughter, Luise, played with her dolls in the corner of the room and had funny nicknames bestowed on her by the poet when she made too much noise. In addition, there were the Meyers, with whom Schiller continued on excellent terms, and a younger sister of Frau Meyer; there were the actors Heinrich Beck and his wife Karoline Ziegler, both of whom played rôles by Schiller. Schiller had been an angry witness of the difficulties which the clergy placed in the path of their marriage, because Beck was a Protestant and Karoline Ziegler a Catholic; then, in July 1784, the highly talented young actress died at the birth of her first child, and the Catholic priest refused burial to the wife of a Protestant: which of course provided the author of *Don Carlos* with still deeper shades of black for his Domingos and his Grand Inquisitors. There was Iffland, for whose skill as a playwright Schiller had a boundless admiration, although there was always an element of uncertainty about his personal relationship with him. And finally there was Charlotte von Kalb, born Baroness Marschalk von Ostheim, a relative of the Wolzogens, who became very intimate with Schiller.

Nothing definite is known about the nature of this or any other of the relationships with women which Schiller formed while in Mannheim, which leaves all the more room for sur-

* Lessing was Librarian at Wolfenbüttel in Brunswick at the time.
† See p. 100f.

mise. That in addition to his professional and financial worries he also had to endure a lover's cares, is a fact that emerges from a letter written from Jena in 1789, when he recalls how in Mannheim he 'wandered around, a poor fool with a wretched passion in his breast'. And he wrote to Goethe in 1796 of his admiration for the latter's realistic description in *Wilhelm Meister** of the goings-on and the love-life of a theatre. 'I am a very competent judge of such things, being better acquainted with both than I have cause to wish.' But these passages can hardly be applied to Margarethe Schwan, even less to Charlotte von Kalb. The latter has been involved in such conjectures because of a Schiller poem *Freigeisterei der Leidenschaft (Free-thinking Passion)*. There is talk in it of a 'titanic struggle of duty', of love for another's wife, of happiness almost snatched and finally renounced; the subtitle, which points to 'Laura' and the year 1782, was thought to be a tactful deception, and the poem was taken to refer to Frau von Kalb. If that is the case, then one has reason, when reading the memoirs which Charlotte dictated as a blind old lady, to be grateful to the poet's guardian angel for having preserved him from such a connection. She is the same woman who later was the friend of Jean Paul and who took Hölderlin into her house as her son's private tutor, so she cannot have been devoid of intellectual and human qualities; but her papers make it quite clear that her character was somewhat insubstantial and insipid, and indeed contained a good deal of insincerity and melting sentimentality.

She had been married since October 1783. Her husband was an officer in the service of the French, and was garrisoned at Landau, where there was a French occupation force at the time. French officers in garrison were not allowed to live with their families, so Charlotte lived in Mannheim, where Kalb visited her from time to time, and where she bore a son in September 1784. She was, therefore, frequently alone, and spiritually unsatisfied by the husband she had not chosen herself but had had foisted upon her by her uncle and guardian. Her acquaintance-

* Cf. 37, note.

ship with Schiller was through the recommendation of Frau von Wolzogen. He read to her from *Don Carlos*, and she seems by frank criticism to have cured him, at least for a time, of his habit of exaggerated declamation. For when, at Christmas 1784, he travelled to the Court of Darmstadt, with a letter of introduction from Charlotte to a friend of hers who was a lady at court, in order to present himself to Duke Karl August of Weimar, the protector of all higher culture in Germany, and was called upon by the Duke to read the first act of his new work, Schiller found that, in complete contrast to that unfortunate reading of *Fiesko* in Mannheim, he had a very appreciative audience; and Karl August appointed him 'Councillor in the service of Weimar' by autograph letter – 'I wish thereby to give you a token of my esteem.'

In his biography of Schiller, Reinhard Buchwald points out that in Mannheim Schiller became thoroughly familiar with the copies of Classical statuary in the Academy of Art, and says that for Schiller this study was 'not a solitary impulse, but the beginning of a lifelong preoccupation of the greatest urgency and fruitfulness'. And in fact this was one of the decisive experiences of the Mannheim years, an experience of physical contemplation with a powerful after-effect which must be rated very important, following as it did upon a conception of Antiquity which he had based solely on its intellectual and moral reflection in the works of historians (Plutarch, Sallust and Suetonius). The Mannheim collection was famous, both Goethe and Lessing had visited it; but what Friedrich Schiller derived from it was completely characteristic of the man. 'Why do all the rhetorical and representational arts of Antiquity aim so much at ennoblement? Man here achieved something that was more than he himself was, that makes one think of something greater than its own species.' With rapturous gaze lingering on the torso of Herakles at rest, he says – and one can almost hear the delight in his words – 'that these people believed in truth and beauty because one from amongst them felt truth and beauty; because they were a noble race, because virtue and beauty are but sisters born of the same mother'. He had been touched by the maternal blessing of nature and made to feel that not everything the spirit boldly demands should remain merely an idea, a longing: it should seek its realization. He had had more than enough bitter experiences amongst men; here he learned a new courage with which to face this divinely created world.

More than enough bitter experiences. Schiller had been unable to deliver the stipulated third play, *Don Carlos*, and so the theatrical contract which expired in September was not extended. In November there was a meeting of the Theatre Committee, in which Schiller no longer took part. One may presume that Dalberg thought himself completely in the right and was quite unable to see his actual crime: that the contract had been unfavourable and the salary inadequate, that he had aroused expectations in the poet and assumed a human responsibility for his fate, and so had no right to drop him as he did and expose him to the intrigues of the town and the theatrical world. It even happened that at a rehearsal Schiller was faced with open insubordination and rudeness on the part of the actors. 'The very least token of respect that an actor can show his author is to memorize his lines. Even this modest demand has not been met in my case,' complains Schiller to Dalberg. 'Once these gentlemen of ours have a mastery over the language, then they will be able if necessary to help out their indolence with extemporization. . . . It is my hope and belief that an author who has put three plays on the stage, amongst them *Die Räuber*, has some right to reprove lack of respect.' One can sense that the break has occurred and is irreparable. It was now planned that a periodical *Rheinische Thalia* (*The Rhenish Thalia*) should provide Schiller with the means of support. However, the theatre, to which it was offered as a 'Mannheim Dramaturgy' (corresponding to the one Lessing had written for Hamburg)* would hear nothing of the undertaking, and Schwan, too, who

---

* Lessing was theatre-critic attached to the Hamburg theatre from 1767–69. His *Hamburg Dramaturgy* started as a day-to-day criticism of performances, but soon developed into a general discussion of the plays themselves and of wider

could have found in it an opportunity of rendering effective assistance, refused publication and would only undertake commission. Schiller therefore decided to publish it himself. He was encouraged to do this by the continued steady sales of his books, which brought *him* in, of course, nothing but the outright advance fee, while further editions benefited only the publisher – and the pirates. There was no law in those days to protect the author from the theft of the products of his own mind by unauthorized copying. In the periodical published under his own name he would gather his public together – 'forge a bond of friendship,' as he puts it, 'between the public and myself' – and to this end he hit upon a bold and natural device: in the announcement of *Rheinische Thalia* he told the readers the story of his youth.

A fanfare opens the proceedings: 'I write as a citizen of the world, who serves no monarch.' Then he describes his incarceration in the *Karlsschule* and his passion for literature, which 'is as fiery and powerful as first love'. He characterizes his unwieldy first play as 'an example of an offspring brought into the world through the unnatural cohabitation of subordination and genius. *Die Räuber* cost me my family and my fatherland . . . in the midst of my enjoyment of the first seductive praise which, unexpected and undeserved, reached me from the remotest provinces, I was forbidden in my place of birth, on pain of fortress arrest, to write. My decision is well known – I shall remain silent about the rest, because in no circumstances do I consider it proper to indulge in hostility towards one who up till then had been a father to me. My example shall pluck no leaf from the laurels of a prince whom all the ages will name. His school has made the fortune of many hundreds, even if it failed to make my own.'

If a situation which is at once politically and humanly difficult has to be brought to the attention of the public, it could not be

---

questions of dramaturgical interest. Among other things discussed are the true nature of Aristotelian catharsis, and the superiority of Shakespeare to French Classical tragedy.

done more nobly or with a more attractive and child-like worldly wisdom than here. There is nobility and wisdom, too, in the way in which he now stepped before his audience; in just such a way, in his last great work *Demetrius*,* the young Demetrius would stand before the Diet at Cracow: 'Now all my connections have been dissolved. The public is now everything – my study, my sovereign, my confidant . . . a feeling of greatness comes over me at the thought of wearing no other shackle but the claim of the world – of appealing to no other throne but the human spirit. . . .'

It was in March 1785 when these confessions in the first number of the *Thalia* made their way into the world. We find that Schiller had already turned all his thoughts and hopes away from Mannheim. 'Men and circumstances, heaven and earth are all repugnant to me,' he wrote to his friends in Leipzig, whose communication he finally answered in December, begging their indulgence for the inexcusable delay; thereafter he kept up a lively correspondence with them. Körner had issued a pressing invitation to come to Leipzig, and trusting in the genuine friendly sympathy he sensed here, Schiller now made a direct request for assistance, for release from his difficulties in Mannheim. For his debts had piled up there as well, and he needed money to free himself from them and make an honourable departure from the town. He asked them to procure him an advance of 300 thalers from a bookseller; he would pay back fifty every two months, at whatever rate of interest was customary in the State, from the proceeds of the *Thalia* (which, of course, had not yet materialized). Or else, if a Leipzig bookseller would take over publication of the *Thalia*, 'I should soon be out of the embarrassment.' The publisher Göschen was induced to do this by Körner; they spared Schiller the knowledge that it was Körner himself who put up the money.

A long tribulation had been overcome. Now he could breathe more freely. 'Leipzig appears in my dreams as the rosy dawn behind the wooded hills.' We know almost nothing about

* See below, p. 184-7.

his Mannheim farewells. The first intimation of the closeness of his relations with Margarethe Schwan comes in the letter, one of the first written from Leipzig, in which he asks the book-seller for his daughter's hand. Schwan is said to have replied in the negative, but he himself later maintained that he left the decision to her, and it caused him considerable surprise that nothing came of the whole affair. From Charlotte von Kalb's memoirs one can merely deduce that she wished to persuade Schiller to remain and was unwilling to lose his society. She seems to have been unable to grasp his material difficulties.

On April 9, 1785, Schiller left Mannheim, having spent the last evening with Streicher. The latter's path led him first to Augsburg, where he married, and then to Vienna, where he lived as a piano-maker and composer and had classical oratorios performed. He died there a respected citizen in 1833. The time he spent in Mannheim in Schiller's company remained for his whole life a shining memory. In 1795 he wrote once more to Schiller and received a most cordial reply. When he wrote and published his memoirs after Schiller's death, he did it in order to devote the proceeds to a memorial for his great friend. But now in Mannheim, after a long conversation about God and the world and a poet's wretched lot, and how a man of ability should be able to make his way, they shook hands on the promise 'that neither would write to the other until he [Schiller] was a government minister, and the other a *Kapellmeister*'. It was a solemn promise, and partly a joke; for a farewell is easier if made in a jesting spirit.

CHAPTER VI

LEIPZIG AND *DON CARLOS*
(1785-88)

*

A broad clear brow, eyes with no trace of guile in them, a mouth that is good-tempered yet firm – that is how Gottfried Körner looks in the portrait by Anton Graff. His father, a superintendent and preacher at St Thomas's Church, died in 1787 and left him in comfortable circumstances; he had enjoyed a good education, had travelled in Germany, England, France and Switzerland, and at thirty-three was already a Commissioner of the Ecclesiastical Consistory and at the same time the assessor of an economic delegation in Dresden. Although his was not a mind that sheds a light of its own on the world around him, he was still a faithful mirror of the light he received, a man whose judgment saw a work of art as a whole and never lost sight of essentials through concentration upon the trimmings, a danger that threatened Romantic criticism, for all its brilliance, a generation later. We have already seen how surely, in his very first letter, Körner grasped the essential quality of Schiller's art, and then how he was able to offer concealed assistance. To watch Schiller moving from Streicher to Körner, from one faithful friend to another, is to receive a comforting remainder of the lives of the ancient heroes, whom every so often the gods allow to shelter with some hospitable king, from whom they receive care and attention, and where they are strengthened for their next labour.

When Schiller arrived in Leipzig on April 17, 'shattered and broken by a journey quite without parallel in my experience, for the way to you, dear friends, is as wretched and miserable as they say the way to Heaven is', Körner was not there, detained by his duties in Dresden. Young Huber received him and took him to Minna and Dora Stock. Dora was the livelier of the two sisters, quick of eye and of understanding, while Minna was quiet and feminine, the little mother and protective genius of the household. Both were a little nervous of the poet, whom they imagined to be like Moor the robber, but he turned out to be 'a fair-haired, timid young man, with tears in his eyes, who scarcely dared to address us. Yet at this very first visit his shyness abated, and he never tired of repeating to us how grateful he was, and that we had made him the happiest man under the sun'.

Ludwig Ferdinand Huber was really too young to be engaged to Dora, who was four years his senior. They later broke off their engagement. Perhaps her sharp and ready tongue was partly to blame, but the Körners and Schiller as well took his unfaithfulness amiss, and it was not until his early death that their friend's image, distorted through the quarrel, was once more seen in focus. Huber was of mixed blood. His mother was a Parisian, but his father – at that time a Lecturer in French at Leipzig – was the son of a Bavarian peasant; he had found his way to Paris in his youth and had led a literary existence in the Diderot circle. Ludwig Ferdinand Huber had a good brain and was also destined to have a successful career as a writer – he was, incidentally, the first of Kleist's contemporaries to recognize immediately the genius in his early work *Die Familie Schroffenstein* (*The Schroffenstein Family*) when it appeared anonymously in 1803, and wrote an appreciation of it in a review.

In Leipzig Schiller enjoyed first of all the bustle of the town with its Fair, and was brought into contact with many artists and writers, such as the painter Reinhart; he also met here his friend from Frankfurt am Main, Sophie Albrecht. He developed a personal friendship with Göschen, whose firm at that time was publishing the first collected edition of Goethe's writings and who, by taking over the *Thalia*, had also become Schiller's publisher. In May they all set off to spend their summer holidays in Gohlis, where Göschen lived in the same room with Schiller, while Dora and Minna dwelt in a cottage nearby, and Huber not far away. 'I cannot describe to you,' reports Göschen in a letter, 'how grateful and accommodating [Schiller] is when given critical advice, and how much he labours at his own moral perfection. . . . He knew that Moritz [the author of *Anton Reiser*] had reviewed him very spitefully in a Berlin newspaper, but nevertheless he received [him] during his stay here with such respect and such engaging politeness that on his departure Moritz embraced him and promised eternal friendship. . . . Schiller has often admonished myself, Huber and Körner with the greatest seriousness, indeed with overwhelming eloquence, to exert all our powers to become men whom the world will one day be sorry to lose. We all owe him a great deal, and in the hour of my death I shall remember him with joy.'

That meeting with Karl Philipp Moritz was actually the first occasion on which an understanding was reached with the world of Goethe, for Moritz's objections to Schiller's early plays proceeded from an aesthetic closely related to Goethe's own, and in which they were soon to come still closer while Goethe and Moritz were together in Rome.*

The circle of Körner's friends assembled on July 1 at a property situated five hours from Leipzig, the residence of some relatives: and here for the first time Schiller and Körner met face to face. The next day – it was Körner's birthday – the poet travelled back to Gohlis with Huber and Göschen, filled with thoughts of the perfectibility of human life, and of how he himself, through the hostility of fate and his own fault, had neglected this task and had 'misused the past with dire waste'; when he and his travelling-companions walked into an inn to drink Huber's health, all three were touched by what seemed

---

* Karl Philipp Moritz (1756–93) combined academic and editorial activities, and is chiefly famous for his autobiographical novel *Anton Reiser* (1785–90), a faithful portrait of the middle-class pietism of the day and of his own character and abortive struggles to become an actor. He developed an interest in mythology, and met Goethe in Rome in 1786.

to them to be the breath of the beyond. 'We looked at each other in silence, our mood was one of solemn devotion, and each of us had tears in his eyes which he sought to suppress. Göschen confessed that he could still feel the wine burning in all his limbs, Huber's face was red as fire as he admitted that he had never had such a good wine, and I myself felt as if I were at the beginning of the Communion Service. . . . I heard the organ and stood before the altar. And then, for the first time, it flashed across our minds that today was your birthday. Without knowing it we had held a sacred celebration of it.'

This passage from Schiller's letter is sure to make a disagreeable impression on Christian readers, for the divine and human spheres are here illicitly intermingled. But, equally, one cannot fail to recognize that the scene – which is curiously reminiscent of the significant opening scene in Gerhard Hauptmann's novel *Der Narr in Christo* (*The Fool in Christ*) – affords a glimpse into the inmost world of Schiller's mind. Schiller had begun as a pietist, and the Enlightenment had awakened and formed his mind. The result could only be secularization: friendship between human beings took the place of the sacrament in which the God-man communicates Himself to His own people. But to the theologians who lift a warning finger at this point one must reply in all seriousness that if they had been able to preserve the mystery of the Divine Presence in their services, the life of the community would have been irradiated by it, and such a secularization would never have taken place. In Schiller's 'sacred fire' of human friendship there lies, albeit discoloured and misdirected, more *piety* than in the precision of theological definitions which are lacking in heart. Idealistic humanism wants to make man holy. It errs in thinking that this can be accomplished by human power. But even greater guilt attached to that 'enlightened' religiosity which had abandoned the attempt to sanctify man, and was content to make him moral. And something further must be considered: in the thought and feeling of German Classicism those elements of sanctification are everywhere present, determined, in Schiller's case by the intellect, in Goethe's by nature. Their substance is still Christian, if not the forms in which it is expressed, and we should realize that, having escaped from the world of these classical forms, we have now been given a new chance of acquiring their Christian substance and applying it to present-day problems. I consider that schools, literary criticism and the theatre have scarcely yet perceived their task, have done practically nothing about it. But such opportunities are only given within a limited historical context, and can be missed.

According to Körner's testimony, it was in Gohlis that Schiller wrote his *An die Freude (Ode to Joy)*; it is the High Song* of this group of friends. But from the first moment of its existence, this whole age, with its enthusiasm and belief in man, recognized its own reflection in it, an age on the eve of the Great Revolution, which wanted to change everything and create a paradise on earth. Transcripts were circulated even before the poem was printed in the *Thalia*; it was sung wherever young people came together; Körner himself, and several others after him, set it to music, until it reached its consummation in Beethoven's ninth symphony:

> Seid umschlungen, Millionen!
> Diesen Kuß der ganzen Welt!
> Brüder – überm Sternenzelt
> Muß ein lieber Vater wohnen.†

It is the childlike spirit of Germany singing a welcome to freedom, to France and to a new dawn for humanity – but what came instead was war and subjugation, which spread like a flood over the German lands. And just as Beethoven, after Bonaparte had made himself Emperor, angrily expunged the dedication from his *Eroica*, so also Kleist was to make a terrible retraction of Schiller's *An die Freude* in his battle-song *Germania an ihre Kinder (Germania to her Children)*. Kleist's ode is planned

---

* *das Hohelied.* : usually applied to the Song of Songs.
 † 'Be embraced, ye millions! This kiss is for the whole world! Brothers – above the starry firmament a loving father surely dwells.'

as a conscious counterpart; it has the same metre, the same verse-form (in both poems an eight-line stanza is answered by a four-line chorus); lines filled with despair depict the misery and scorn which the foreigners have inflicted on his nation, and in place of the praise of joy 'which all beings drink' there now stands hatred expressed in the wild exaggeration of ghastly images. It is frightening to compare the two odes in detail and to see how, in passage after passage, the later poet answers the earlier in a gloomy litany. But it is not sufficient to accuse Kleist and his *furor teutonicus*; instead, one must recognize in the very wildness of his hymn of hate what a shining faith in humanity was here betrayed, buried and destroyed. Were the story of this disappointment not so painful, one might congratulate the theologians on such a striking demonstration of the fact that man can only do evil to man, nation can only do evil to nation, as soon as the vault of an order based on divine sanction is broken.

On August 7, 1785, Körner married Minna, and Schiller celebrated the event in a long, weak poem. 'Only that wife brings happiness who lives for you alone, and with a sincere heart cleaves lovingly to you,' it runs. Few were less at ease in verse than Schiller when the subject afforded him no space in which to unfold his eagle's pinions for a lofty flight. But humour, when he goes in voluntary search of it, does not elude him. Körner had travelled to Dresden with his wife and sister-in-law, and Schiller also arrived there on September 1. The next day he moved with the family to the vineyard at Loschwitz, where Körner had acquired a country-house. Huber followed a few weeks later. Several poetic jests bear witness to the gaiety of their life together, which are precious on account of their rarity in Schiller's work; for example, the *Most Humble Memorandum to Commissioner Körner's Female Laundry Deputation, Submitted by a Depressed Tragic Poet*,* who on the occasion of the great shirt-wash was disturbed while working on a scene from *Don Carlos*;

---

* *'Untertänigste Promemoria an die Konsistorialrat Körnerische weibliche Wasch-deputation, eingerichtet von einem niedergeschlagenen Trauerspieldichter'.*

and later the pretty, dramatized birthday-joke for Körner, in which it is graphically shown how a hundred distractions prevent the harassed man from finding five minutes by himself.

Among Schiller's products of that period is a drama, *Der Menschenfeind* (*The Misanthropist*), born of his bitter experiences in Mannheim; however, the subject was not, as in Shakespeare's *Timon of Athens*,* taken as a tragic myth of human existence, but was treated philosophically. It remained a fragment. To this period belong also the sketch of a philosophical correspondence, *Julius and Raphael*, in which Körner was to be his partner, and the important story *Der Verbrecher aus verlorener Ehre* (*The Man turned Criminal through Loss of Honour*). The latter had been preceded as early as 1782 by Schiller's first attempt at narrative, *Eine großmütige Handlung aus der neuesten Geschichte* (*A Generous Deed from Recent History*). It was to be followed by the novel *Der Geisterseher* (*The Visionary*), the beginning of which in the *Thalia* so excited his contemporaries that Schiller was pestered for years by readers' letters demanding a continuation of the book. Finally, the last of his narrative writings, and the masterpiece, is the *Novelle, Spiel des Schicksals* (*A Game of Fate* – 1789). With this story and the criminal-tale about the landlord of the Sun the modern German *Novelle*† is born. Kleist, whose *Michael Kohlhaas* is closely related thematically to the tale of the landlord of the Sun, could do no more than complete what Schiller had already begun. What the German language learns in this work, or rather, what out of its fullness it presents to the master-craftsman, is the controlled, dammed-up utterance by means of which an event seems to transmit itself without any commentary. The sum total of the conceptual meaning is condensed into the rhythm which determines the sequence of the sentences; it is, in truth, the *tone* as well that makes the *Novelle*. *Spiel des*

---

* A play with which Schiller was much preoccupied during the Mannheim years.

† The *Novelle* is a story of medium length and characteristic structure (with a tendency to revolve round some striking, possibly symbolical central event) which became the form most favoured by German writers during the middle of the nineteenth century.

Schicksals concerns the life-story of a man whom Schiller himself had met at home. His rise to the rank of Minister and to a position of dominance over his own prince is described with terse, incomparably sure strokes; then follows his fall, a terrible imprisonment, liberation at last; and then, written as if in letters of forged steel, the conclusion: 'He died as commander of the fortress of X, where prisoners of state are kept. One might expect that towards these he exercised a humanity the value of which he must have learnt on his own person. But he treated them in a harsh and capricious manner, and it was an outburst of rage against one of them that stretched him in his coffin in his eightieth year.' This little-read story is perhaps particularly suitable for correcting the shallow notion of Schiller's so-called 'idealism' which is current today.

The chief poetic product of the Dresden period was *Don Carlos*, which reached maturity only gradually, and with greater difficulty than any of the earlier plays. The difficulty rose particularly from the fact – as Schiller later confided to the public with characteristic frankness in his *Letters concerning 'Don Carlos'* – that 'the work had of necessity to share in the various vicissitudes that my manner of thinking and feeling has undergone [during the long interval since the first draft] . . . New ideas ousted the earlier ones; Carlos himself had fallen in my favour, perhaps for no other reason than that I was so many years ahead of him, and for the opposite reason Marquis Posa had taken his place'. The play's centre of gravity had shifted; from a 'family portrait in a princely house', which is how Schiller had still described it to Dalberg in 1784, it had become a play 'expressing a view of life'.* It went to the core of the age, fighting in the front rank of its spiritual battles: the scene between the King and Posa was written in Dresden. And at this point a further shift of emphasis took place, perhaps without the poet's noticing it himself at first. Because Posa appears to be so completely the spokesman of his age and shares its errors as well as its enthusiasms, those great discussions about domi-

* See synopsis, p. 199.

nion and liberty were felt at the end of the nineteenth and the beginning of the twentieth centuries to be outdated, and it was insufficiently realized with what massive weight Philipp, a great man experienced and grown old in the trade of kingship, is opposed to the 'strange enthusiast'. It is indeed possible that this royal portrait issued from a level of Schiller's intuition of the nature of things that had not yet fully emerged into consciousness; for every spectator senses how Schiller's passion for liberty turns the words to fire on Posa's lips. His intellect sided with Posa and wanted to rush us into a similar partisanship. But Schiller was more than just an advocate of the ideas of his age: he was a dramatist and a poet, one of the greatest who have ever lived. His poetic intuition was like a spontaneous light in his hands, shining deep into the intricate tensions of which the real world consists. It illuminates the countenance of the aged king, and now the poet *sees*, and makes us see, what it means to have to rule and at the same time to be a man, and that freedom alone cannot build a state. For freedom and sovereignty are mutually conditioned, and only the constant struggle between them, in which the scales reach a quivering equilibrium, makes a true political life possible, and then only for a brief span which must again and again be fought for and won.

When this insight was granted him, Schiller had changed from a youth into a man. It is the reality of events, it is history, which here opposes the would-be reformer. In the following years we shall find him engaged in the objective study and delineation of history.

In *Don Carlos* there is a marvellous mixture of riper wisdom with the youthful brilliance which suffuses so many of the scenes, a mingling of tones and colours that makes the play unique in the whole range of Schiller's works. Precisely because it represents his first venture into a new field, it contains more striking weaknesses than either of the two dramas that preceded it. The change of plan made for lack of clarity in the composition, which was otherwise Schiller's greatest strength; artificial linkings are frequently necessary in order to bring

together things that are really out of harmony with one another
– for example, Posa's intrigue to save Carlos, which ends in an
almost boastfully heroic self-sacrifice. Schiller tried to refute
the objections – but even if they remain valid, they are trans-
cended by the triumphant power of his art, which lives through
its verve, through the power of its scenes: not only Posa and
Philipp, but also the conversation of the young men, Princess
Eboli, the audience with the admiral who had commanded the
shattered Armada, and all the scenes with the Queen, of which
the most beautiful is her dismissal of Posa when he goes to his
death; but there are also Philip's tears for Posa, and the Grand
Inquisitor, the petrified mask of power, who has killed freedom
and can now no longer be reached by any human sound. But
the power of these scenes on the stage is transmitted by the
language, Schiller's language, just as Wagner's power derives
from his music. The modern stage seems to be no longer aware
of this fact, otherwise the language would be more carefully
handled. For the first time (Goethe's verse-*Iphigenia* not yet
having appeared)* German dramatic blank verse rings out,
vibrant, full-blooded and yet handled with complete freedom.
As used by Lessing in *Nathan der Weise* (*Nathan the Wise* –
1779) it still had a certain dry, serene quality, lit by intellect;
Schiller was the first to make it an expression of the human soul
with its intuitions and its dreams. Schröder, the manager of the
Hamburg theatre, had an ear for it; although the poet himself
offered him a prose adaptation, he decided in favour of the
iambic version and on August 27, 1787, gave it its first performance, which was a pronounced success. At the same time
Schiller declined Schröder's invitation to come to Hamburg as
resident playwright, which shows how heavily his experiences
in Mannheim still weighed upon him; but it also shows him
realizing that his future tasks will lead him in a different
direction.

'The boyhood of our spirit is past,' we read in a letter to
Huber in 1785. 'I love the beautiful, ethereal ability to take fire

---

* Goethe's *Iphigenia auf Tauris* (cf. 37, note) was first written in prose.

over some great decision. It belongs to the higher man, but it does not itself perfect him. Enthusiasm is the bold thrust that propels the ball into the air . . . the ball describes an arc, for its force is broken in the air. . . . But this arc, too, is so beautiful!' A moving utterance which really, as he himself says, hints symbolically at the fate of all human plans. It became increasingly clear to him that he could not remain within the charmed circle of his friends, dependent on the support which Körner so magnanimously offered; instead, he must take the reins into his own hands. A man should not let himself be sheltered from storm and flood; an island provides a welcome rest and refuge, but then the barque must put out into open water again, for the current flows on. Schiller received much help from friends; when he did, he was grateful and happy for the gift. But he was free from the notion of a later age that great talents have a natural right to claim shelter from the battle of life, which, after all, ultimately has a weakening effect and is harmful to their work.

We do not need to follow in detail the gradual ripening of his decision to leave Dresden. Intellectual and social conditions there made their contribution – a town in which the court lived a life of dull and superficial piety, while the opera and drama were hampered by petty censorship. What help were the fine pictures and the beautiful countryside, thought Schiller, if one had at the same time to live in an 'intellectual desert'?

But, for all that, not a desert of the heart. In February 1787 the Körners, together with Huber and Schiller, attended a grand masked ball, and the latter fell violently in love with a young beauty, Henriette von Arnim. She was certainly not the selfish and superficial creature that malicious gossip declared her to be; but she was 'of good family', and there could be no thought of a union with the poet in Dresden. She later made two suitable marriages, but cherished Schiller's memory and also his letters, and only burnt these at her death, for what was in them was for her alone. Love may mean great happiness, but writing is laborious; and *Don Carlos*, the book version of which

G

was already being set in type though it still lacked an ending, looked like being abandoned. But then Körner took over the rôle of a beneficent literary providence and rented rooms for the poet in the isolated little town of Tharandt, away from the firing-line. Schiller was supposed to write, and write he did. He was only allowed to receive letters from his beloved. 'These accursed, pretty letters have completely addled my brain. The soup looks languishingly at me, and my landlord simply cannot understand how one can let one's food get cold over a letter.' One can hear what is happening: the patient is making fun of himself, which means he is on the road to recovery. The upshot of the affair was that he parted from Henriette.

In the June of 1787 Schiller read the concluding acts of *Don Carlos*, which had been finished in Tharandt, to the Körner circle. When he set off for Weimar the next month, it was planned that he should first of all refresh the Weimar Duke's memory of him, then travel on to Hamburg in order to see *Don Carlos* performed and make the personal acquaintance of Schröder, and finally – no date was set – that he should return to his friends in Dresden. On July 20 he drove out through the gate.

CHAPTER VII

WEIMAR AND MARRIAGE
(1789-90)

*

Karl August of Weimar had gone away to Potsdam: Schiller missed him by an hour at the coaching-station in Naumburg. It would have been useful to have an informal conversation with him, but nobody knew when he would return to his capital, which Schiller himself reached on July 21, 1787. There the only person who was expecting him was Charlotte von Kalb, who had spent a lonely winter on her estate and was now having her eyes treated in Weimar by a local doctor, Hufeland. Her presence was another reason for Schiller's journey to Weimar, and he spent the very first evening with her. 'Our reunion,' he reported to Körner, 'had such a constraining, numbing effect on me, that I find it impossible to describe it to you. Charlotte has remained just the same, except for a few traces of indisposition which, however, the expectancy and excitement of reunion effaced for the evening, and which I can only observe today. The strange thing was that from the very moment of our being together I felt just as if it had only been yesterday that I left her, so familiar was everything about her, so quickly did we pick up the broken threads of our relationship.'

One can see that she appropriated him with a kind of passion, even though only as an 'intellectual companion'. But she wanted to show off her property as well. 'We have resolved,' wrote Schiller, 'to make no secret of our relationship,' and Weimar, where people were already accustomed to such things, evinced respectful interest. Goethe was still in Italy, but Charlotte von

Kalb was acquainted with the Dowager Duchess and the Duchess Luise, as well as with Wieland and Herder. Schiller announced himself to these two in respectful letters, as befitted a young writer addressing famous fellow authors, and both received him in a friendly manner.

From Stuttgart he had already sent a copy of *Die Räuber* to Wieland, a Swabian like himself, and afterwards, through the mediation of Schwan, had exchanged letters and greetings. Schiller stumbled over 'a press of delightful little creatures, children ranging in size from small to minute', when he entered Wieland's house. The master of the house, who was in his fifty-fourth year, was the most important writer of the German Rococo and was gifted with that 'delicacy, daintiness, comprehensibility, and natural elegance' of which Goethe says that 'it is not to be attained through effort, but through serene, inspired attentiveness'. But Wieland's mind did not remain a prisoner of his own ornamental garden. As editor of the *Der teutsche Merkur* (*The German Mercury*) he was obliged to concern himself with whatever new literature emerged. Even though he noticed Schiller's lack of 'correction, purity, taste, delicacy', which the latter himself held to be virtues worth striving for, he had nevertheless been quick to sense Schiller's importance, and would later be the only person in Weimar to take an interest in the young Kleist, have him as his guest and recognize in him a kinsman of Shakespeare and Sophocles; so he must also be credited with an 'inspired attentiveness' to things that were foreign to his nature.

A different atmosphere surrounded Herder. He was forty-three, looked like an Italian abbé, and his conversation was full of fire and intellect, but 'he treated me like a person of whom one only knows that he is supposed to be somebody. It is my opinion that he has read nothing by me'. Schiller found him 'astoundingly polite, one feels at ease in his presence', and he sensed his seriousness; but it would have been asking too much of a man not yet twenty-eight years old, who had the strenuous task before him of bringing his youthful promise to fruition, to expect him to grasp the tragedy of the great awakener who had sown such fertile seed, but was to see the harvest gathered by others, and end in bitterness and solitude.

Karl August's mother, the widowed Duchess Anna Amalia, was the real founder of Weimar's intellectual fame. It was through her that Wieland had been brought to the court as the prince's tutor, and thus a beginning made of that dense constellation that shone in their small firmament. Through Wieland, Schiller was introduced to her court at Tiefurt, and on a further occasion she had the 'gallantry' to invite him together with Charlotte von Kalb to supper and a concert. The Duchess was friendly, but Schiller quickly perceived that her notion of great poetry was derived from the clipped formality of the French style, and reacted with defiant self-assertiveness. Unluckily Gotter, his adversary of Mannheim days, also turned up in Weimar; he had the reputation of being a good reciter, and read *Don Carlos*, with unfavourable comments, in Tiefurt, without Schiller's being present. The play found its only advocate there in Herder. When the reigning Duchess Luise appeared again in Weimar after an absence, Schiller was so fed up with the life of the court that he did not even have himself presented. He was thinking of leaving.

Leaving? Quitting the field? Was it not precisely here that he must win the contest? Goethe's name is at first mentioned only incidentally in Schiller's reports to Körner, but the thought of him is always in the background. He is sunning himself amid the beauties of the south, thought Schiller, whilst I have to drag myself from one wearisome task to the next. And everyone spoke of him 'in a worshipping kind of way'; with Herder one could scarcely speak of anything else. He has a universal understanding and deep feeling; he had never consciously pursued anyone, never undermined another's happiness; what he was, he was totally. Like Julius Caesar he could be many things at once. Schiller had been advised to seek the acquaintanceship of Major von Knebel, who was an intimate friend of Goethe's and had great influence with the Duke. The latter's younger brother, Prince Konstantin, had been taught by him. Schiller found Knebel 'scornful of all speculative thought, and attached to nature to the point of affectation'. Here Schiller encountered Goethe's faith in nature in a form which could hardly please him in its sectarian exaggeration. But he tried hard to get on with Knebel, and on August 28 he was invited by him to Goethe's garden, where a small company celebrated the birthday of their absent friend. 'We had a good feed, and I drank to Goethe's health in Rhenish. He can hardly have imagined in Italy that I was one of his guests at home, but fate plays strange tricks.' And almost like a schoolboy anxious to show that he is not impressed, Schiller adds: 'After the meal we found the garden illuminated, and a quite tolerable firework display brought the evening to a close.'

He also made the acquaintance of Frau von Stein. She could never have been beautiful, he thought, 'but her face has a gentle seriousness and a very characteristic openness'; he understood how she could mean so much to Goethe. On another occasion Corona Schröter, who had once sown great confusion in Goethe's heart, read *Iphigenia* in Goethe's original manuscript version (i.e. the prose one)* to him and Charlotte von Kalb. 'When I saw and heard her reading, I had to think back to the time when she was in her prime and is said to have done the same thing.' For this reason she became 'interesting' to him, and he and Corona were attracted to one another.

So everywhere there stood signposts to Goethe's world, which were attentively read by Schiller. His plans were already laid. There was no longer any question of a journey to Hamburg; he would not leave Weimar. 'I am beginning to feel tolerably at ease, and my method of achieving this is – not to ask after anybody.' For he saw that that was what they all did there. Weimar was a small country town of six thousand inhabitants, many of whom practised a little agriculture, and in the evening cows were driven home through narrow streets which were mostly unpaved. The street lighting was scarcely worth speaking of,

* Cf. 37, note.

and the town was still enclosed by walls, moats and gateways. Each of the educated people there lived in his 'snail's shell', and Schiller, too, could build himself one: his work.

Since the middle of August he had been working at *Die Geschichte des Abfalls der vereinigten Niederlande* (*The History of the Revolt of the United Netherlands*) a full twelve hours a day, sometimes more. His main effort was directed towards gathering and mastering his material; to its presentation he brought what could never be learnt: his eye for 'the great matters of humanity'. The grand manner of recounting them was but the natural consequence of this. However outdated his work may be today in points of factual detail, Schiller here set up a model on which German historical writing in the grand manner is based. It is moving to read what he wrote to Huber at that time: 'We have failed to recognize our great asset: time. A conscientious use of it could make us into something quite amazing.' In the autumn Duke Karl August returned home for a short visit. His tiny state gave him little to do, so he had had himself made a Prussian major-general and as such went to Holland on a politico-military mission. Schiller had his presence announced to him, but added that he only wished to pay his respects, there was nothing else he wished to discuss. He did not wish to be thought of as one of the *beaux exprits* grabbing at court assistance.

But there was a chance of becoming a professor at Jena, where one 'need not bother one's head about the high and mighty'. The historical work, as soon as it was finished, would give him a claim to the post; at Jena he would be near enough to Weimar, and, moreover, an independent person whose work benefited the state. Schiller spent six days in Jena at the house of Professor Reinhold, a son-in-law of Wieland, and of the other professors he met Döderlein, Griesbach and Schütz; the last was the editor of the *Allgemeine Literaturzeitung* (*General Literary News*). He got on particularly well with Reinhold, who made it look as if a summons to Jena was a definite prospect. But for the moment Schiller was unwilling to sacrifice his independent position as a writer. The most significant thing Reinhold did for him was to draw his attention to Kant, on whom Reinhold had advertised a lecture for the coming autumn; in fact, they were all keen Kantians in Jena, and in a dispute between Kant and Herder they rallied round the banner of the man from Königsberg.* Schiller read the latter's treatise, *Idee zu einer allgemeinen Geschichte in weltbürgerlichen Hinsicht* (*Notion of a Universal History in a Cosmopolitan Sense*). It gripped him. 'It seems pretty certain to me that I shall read and perhaps make a study of Kant.'

Since 1786 his sister Christophine had been married to Reinwald and living in Meiningen. Now, as her brother was so near, she begged him urgently and repeatedly to pay them a visit. The invitations to Bauerbach, where Frau von Wolzogen had her son Wilhelm, her daughter Lotte and her fiancé staying with her at the time, were similarly repeated; Schiller was to make the latter's acquaintance, while he already knew Wilhelm Wolzogen from Stuttgart. 'A man who is not completely made of stone finds it impossible to decline everything,' wrote Schiller to Körner, and set out at the end of November 1787 on his duty-trip, little suspecting what happiness it was to bring him. All was well at the Reinwalds': Christophine was completely satisfied with her good, kind hypochondriac. In Bauerbach Schiller expected to rediscover some of the old secret magic of the forest vale that had sheltered him from 1782 to 1783. 'In those days I had not been out into the world, I stood dizzily on its threshold, so to speak, and my imagination had to work quite amazingly hard. Then after five years I returned, not without some experience of people, things and my own self. It was as if the old magic had been blown away. I felt nothing. . . . The language had been lost in which things used to speak to me.'

That is not directed against the people he had known, to whom he remained affectionate and grateful, sentiments which,

---

* Kant spent his whole life in Königsberg, the capital of East Prussia.

when Henriette von Wolzogen died during the following summer, he expressed to her son. What he became conscious of in
Bauerbach was that he had now entered a new period of his life
and thought. Wilhelm von Wolzogen was planning a trip to
Paris. Schiller suggested that he should accompany him to
Weimar, where he could be given useful introductions and
information. Wilhelm agreed, but wished to travel via Rudolstadt, the residency of the little principality of Schwarzburg,
where Frau von Lengefeld lived with her elder daughter Karoline, who had meanwhile married Herr von Beulwitz, and her
younger daughter Lotte. The two girls were cousins of Wilhelm,
for whom he had a tender regard. Schiller and Wolzogen made
the journey on horseback, and found that the Thuringian forest
already showed signs of winter. On a dull day when the two
men, wrapped in their cloaks, rode into the quiet town of Rudolstadt, Karoline and Lotte recognized their cousin Wolzogen,
who jokingly hid half his face in his cloak; they looked curiously
at the other. Not until Wolzogen introduced him did it occur to
them that this was the poet whom they had met briefly in Mannheim in 1784. During the first moments of this second meeting
Schiller, who in his correspondence with Körner had discussed
all sorts of matrimonial projects, found himself thinking: it is
good to be here, let us build tabernacles here; and Lotte asked
herself: has he come for me? – shadowy thoughts, which no
one would have recalled, had not life made them come true.

The gradual growth of their love was not without a touch of
the miraculous, for which reason it should be simply told.
Schiller, whose work called him back to Weimar, only stayed a
day in Rudolstadt this time, but resolved to spend the next
summer in the district, which he thought 'extraordinarily beautiful'. In January 1788, at a masked ball, he unexpectedly found
Lotte standing before him. She had come to Weimar because
her mother wanted to see her presented at court. Soon he began
to write to her, letters full of tender restraint. For it was nice to
dream of marriage and domesticity, but how could he, scarcely
able to support himself, think of providing for two? And even

a poet could see that her mother had other plans for Lotte. He determined to treat the relationship as a purely friendly one. In the middle of May he moved to Volksstädt, near Rudolstadt, where Lotte had found him agreeable quarters in the house of a precentor. During the day he applied himself industriously to his work, but spent the evenings with the Lengefelds. Karoline has left us a description of the exciting time which the sisters, always receptive towards his thoughts and preoccupations, spent with him then; how they breathed a sigh of relief when boring guests had gone, how they then walked towards Volksstädt to meet their friend beneath the beautiful trees on the banks of the Saale, and waited for him on a narrow bridge over the mouth of a forest brook. When they saw him coming towards them through the dusk, 'then our minds found a new, ideal existence opening upon them'. For him, however, the two became a beloved double-image.

Their father had died in 1775. Strangely enough, he, too, like Schiller's father, had been concerned with trees, and just as the latter had set the pattern for planned fruit-growing in his own home, so too Christoph von Lengefeld had given the initial impulse towards a planned and careful management of the German forests. His widow, known to everybody as *chère mère*, occupied a house in the Neue Gasse in Rudolstadt; next door lived Karoline and her husband Beulwitz, a respectable, hard-working civil servant, with whom, however, she was already unhappy. After ten years of marriage, in 1794, she divorced him, against his wishes and those of her mother, and married her old admirer, her cousin Wolzogen. But this marriage did not last either. She had more brilliant gifts than her sister, and even justified reproach is disarmed when, in passing judgment on herself, she says that she did, indeed, wish only to see what was good and right prevail, but that there was a 'mental fastidiousness' in her, 'an urge, even where higher and nobler things were concerned, to have everything done according to my own way of thinking'. Schiller knew instinctively that he needed a tranquil, uncomplicated person as his companion, and in Lotte

106

Lengefeld there was a profound impulse towards self-improvement and a delicate richness of character which was to reach its full flowering through the experience of love. And yet it was always the intense natures like his own that were able to disturb him most; Dora Stock had kindled him a little, as we learn from an admission to Huber, and then he had 'wandered through labyrinths' with Charlotte Kalb which were not without danger – and now once more the lively tempo of Karoline's mind mingled confusingly with the longing for home and security which drew him towards the younger sister.

That summer was to bring his first meeting with Goethe. The Lengefelds knew Goethe, who some time after his return from Italy paid them a Sunday visit in the company of Frau von Stein and several other ladies from Weimar. 'My first sight of him,' wrote Schiller to Körner, 'considerably lowered the high opinion which had been fostered in me of his fine, attractive figure. He is of medium height, rather stiff in his bearing and in his walk as well; his countenance is reserved, but his eye is very expressive . . . one hangs with pleasure on his glance.' In the large gathering it did not come to a personal conversation. 'On the whole, my conception of him, which is in fact a lofty one . . . has not been lowered, but I doubt whether we shall ever come very close to one another. Much that still interests me, that I still have to desire and hope for, has already had its day with him; he is so far ahead of me (less in years than in experience of life and self-development) that we shall never come together again on our respective paths.' Karoline and Lotte, on the other hand, hoped ardently that they would reach an understanding. The barbarian who wrote *Die Räuber* was, after all, now translating Euripides; they had been reading Homer with him the whole summer. He had become a student of the Greeks, which would please Goethe, and the latter must be made aware of the fact. So they left Wieland's *Merkur* on the table, which contained Schiller's most recent poem *Die Götter Griechenlands* (*The Gods of Greece*), and were as pleased as a pair of anglers over a bite when Goethe picked the paper up and asked for the loan of it. He later expressed measured praise: the poem was good, but a little too long.

Nor did Schiller see any reason for expressing unmitigated admiration of Goethe. In a review of *Egmont*, which had just appeared, he praised Goethe's skill in depicting human beings, but thought that the hero was shown too much in moments of human weakness, and called the conclusion, when Liberty (with the features of Klärchen) appears to the sleeping hero, 'a perilous leap into the world of opera'.

In December, when he was once more in Weimar, Schiller suddenly received a decree from the government announcing his appointment for the coming spring as Professor of History at Jena. It was Goethe who sent it to him. Now he had to visit him and thank him. Goethe had been extremely active in the matter, he wrote to Rudolstadt, and very sympathetic towards anything 'that would, in his opinion, contribute to my happiness'. From Schiller's point of view it would have been a project to be considered later, for which his knowledge was as yet inadequate, and its surprising realization robbed him of his freedom. He felt that he had been duped, and struggled with a feeling of bitter disappointment because he observed distinctly that in conversation Goethe was only willing to appear as the benevolent minister, not the poet. And really this favour, like those of the gods, was two-edged. Was not Goethe, in appearing to help him, really thrusting him away? In the course of that winter Schiller wrote a series of very frank confessions to his friends; to Körner he wrote: 'To be near Goethe frequently would make me miserable; even with his closest friends he never has moments of effusion, there is nothing one can grasp him by. . . . He announces his existence through acts of benevolence, but only like a god, without ever making a gift of himself. . . . People should not allow a being like this to grow up anywhere near them. . . . It is a quite remarkable mixture of love and hate that he has aroused in me, a feeling not unlike that which Brutus and Cassius must have had for Caesar; his is a mind that I could cheerfully murder, and then again love with my whole heart. Goethe, too, greatly influences my desire to see my poem completed.' The poem he speaks of here was *Die Künstler* (*The Artists*), which, even more than *An die Freude*, was his most heartfelt song of rejoicing, the expression of his hopes for the age, and an exhortation transcending all ages. He felt that it *must* turn out well, that Goethe *must* recognize its excellence. When Karoline warned him to take his time about fathoming the secret of Goethe's character, he replied: 'I have too much pride and indolence to wait for a man to reveal his character to me. There is one language which all men understand, and that is: use your powers. If each man works with all his might, he cannot remain hidden from his fellows.' And again to Körner: 'I have to laugh when I think back on what I may have written to you about Goethe. You must certainly have seen me in all my weakness, but be that as it may, I am glad to be known by you as I really am. This man, this Goethe, is simply in my path and . . . reminds me so often that fate has dealt hardly with me. How lightly was *his* genius borne along by his fate, and how I have had to fight right up to this very minute! I can no longer catch up all that I have lost . . . but I am still in good heart and believe that things will now take a turn for the better.'

The ominous thing about the Jena affair was that he could expect no fixed salary, only the students' lecture fees. Körner, when he heard this, was not much taken with it and was right in telling him that it was Jena that was making the acquisition, and not he in getting the title of professor. And in the event Schiller found himself obliged to carry on writing for his bread and at the same time to prepare his lectures; this double load of work was to cost him his health. He might still, perhaps, have withdrawn, had he not viewed the job as establishing his claim to future posts and as giving him the opportunity of marriage.

His move to Jena took place in May 1789, and his inaugural lecture was on the twenty-sixth. It was to be anticipated that the students would flock to hear the author of *Die Räuber* on

the subject: *What is and to what end does one study universal history?*
But he did not wish straightaway to ask for the large lecture
hall. It is necessary to make a word-for-word study of his report
to Körner, for he paints a picture of the intellectual youth of
the country, who were to be his own most faithful disciples –
and at the same time conveys his joy at the assent which he felt
was carrying him along. He was right to rejoice in it; for his
speech (there were only two months to go till the outbreak of
the revolution that would change France and the whole world)
contained high and still unbroken hope of the age, but not a
breath of anything calculated to deceive or mislead. Schiller's
lecture-hours – twice weekly – were from six to seven in the
evening. 'By half-past five the lecture room was full. From
Reinhold's window I saw them trooping up the road in a never-
ending stream. Although I was not completely free from nervous-
ness, the growing numbers pleased me, and my courage was
augmented rather than diminished. . . . But gradually the crowd
grew to such an extent that the lobby, floor and steps were
jammed full, and large numbers went away again. Then it occurred to someone who was with me that I might still perhaps
choose another room for this lecture . . . so I proposed that I
should lecture in Griesbach's room. A most amusing panto-
mime now ensued. They all rushed out and poured in a gay
procession down St John's Street, one of the longest in Jena,
which was completely covered in students. Since they ran for
all they were worth in order to get a good seat, the street took
fright. . . . People thought there was a fire-alarm, and in the
castle the guard was roused. 'What's up? What's going on?'
was heard on all sides. So they shouted: 'The new professor is
going to lecture!' So you see that even chance contributed to
the brilliance of my début. I followed . . . accompanied by
Reinhold; I had to walk practically the whole length of the town,
and felt as if I were running the gauntlet. Griesbach's lecture
room is the largest and, when full, can hold between three and
four hundred people. It was full this time, so full that the lobby
and corridor were packed right up to the main door. . . . I could

scarcely find the rostrum, which I mounted amid loud rappings,*
and found myself surrounded by an amphitheatre full of people.
Stuffy though the hall was, on the rostrum it was quite bearable,
for all the windows were open, so that I had fresh air. After the
first ten words I was completely composed. . . . I could still be
heard at the door. My lecture made a great impression: in the
town people talked about it all evening, and from the students
I experienced such attentiveness as had never before been shown
to a new professor. I was treated to a serenade and to three
cheers.'

The summer of 1789 at last brought his affairs of the heart to
a happy resolution. It happened during a short meeting with the
sisters in Lauchstädt, and it was Karoline he had to thank for
it, 'in a moment when the heart experiences the kind of release
which only some kindly genius can bring about'. We know no
more of what went on than these beautiful, reverent words of
hers, written in retrospect. Then followed Schiller's question to
Lotte in the letter of August 3. 'Is it true, dearest Lotte? May I
hope that Karoline has read your heart and from it has given
me the answer which I did not dare to admit to myself?' And
on the fifth followed her answer, with the conclusion that must
have seemed to him like the clear note of a bell: 'Ever your
faithful Lotte.'

The resolving of the triad which had united these three into
the simpler dialogue in which married people must find each
other had not yet been accomplished, though, and was still to
cost them many a heartache before its complete achievement.
Lotte felt that she could never be as much to Schiller as her
sister; her letters only hint with a touching faintness at the
tormenting anxiety which she finally, unable to help herself any
longer, confided to a friend, Karoline von Bacheröden. Karoline
was later to become Wilhelm von Humboldt's wife.† She gave

* German students greet their lecturers by rapping on the desk or stamping
on the floor.
† See pp. 131 ff.

an honest reply which was both sensible and helpful: Lotte should declare herself to Schiller, there could be no doubting the 'sacred truth of his heart'. So it happened, and the tangled threads parted, like a dull day slowly brightening to a clear blue.

In gossip-loving Weimar there could not fail to be talk of Schiller's relations with the Lengefeld family. The news reached Charlotte von Kalb, who had long felt that she was being neglected by him. Hurt by his failure to confide in her, she allowed herself to be carried away by her feelings and said some unfortunate things. Indeed, she now suddenly thought of dissolving her marriage and marrying Schiller, and as a result of her discussions she demanded the return of her letters, which she burnt along with his. Her situation reminds one strangely of that of Charlotte von Stein, who about the same time learned of Goethe's liaison with Christiane and suffered greatly in consequence, although she never wished her relationship with him to be thought of as a possessive love. To bring such a pure relationship about may be difficult; but not until it is about to be lost do all the forces of passion, long declared dead, rise up in protest. We now find Schiller uttering hard words of rejection about Frau von Kalb, which are made comprehensible by her behaviour, for it is probable – even if not demonstrable – that she was the author of an anonymous communication warning Lotte about Schiller. Ten years later *Wallenstein* was performed in Weimar; Frau von Kalb wrote to Schiller expressing her pleasure at the work, and Schiller thanked her in a letter in which he seeks for words that will heal what has passed. Her life ended late, overshadowed and lonely.

On December 18, Schiller wrote to Frau von Lengefeld and asked for the hand of her daughter Lotte. He received a cordial and trusting affirmative, although he could not offer a life of dazzling happiness. His financial circumstances were still very inadequate, the lecture-fees only trickled in, and only through his industry as a writer could he give his wife an existence free of worry. The engagement was now announced to the elder

Schiller, who had been very gratified at his son's appointment
to a professorship, and his blessing was asked. Schiller's mother
was gravely ill at the time, but made a good recovery and read
Lotte's filial letter with great joy. But Schiller had the idea that
a connection with a man of the middle classes like himself might
be made more acceptable to the Lengefelds by a prefix to his
title of Councillor, and he requested the Duke of Meiningen to
create him Privy Councillor: 'such a gift, coming from Your
Grace's hands, would be greatly valued by me'. So Lotte was
to be the wife of a Privy Councillor. The Lengefelds had connections with Karl Theodor von Dalberg, the Coadjutor Bishop
of Erfurt and future Archbishop of Mainz, and the brother of
the director of the Mannheim theatre; he showed the poet
greater understanding and loyalty than did the other. But for
the moment he was unable to help, so the Duke of Weimar had
to be approached for an extra allowance. Karl August felt that
Schiller had for several months now been working for the
University of Jena more or less for nothing; 'in a low voice and
with an embarrassed expression' he told him that 200 thalers
was all he could manage. 'I have taken quite a fancy to your
Duke,' wrote Körner, 'for the way in which he gave you the
salary.'

A slight discord had arisen between the friends because
Schiller was late in confiding the news of his engagement to
Körner. The latter expresses here the kind of reproach that once
Scharffenstein had uttered: 'Some stimulating idea, which gives
rise in you to an intoxicating sense of your own superiority,
displaces . . . at times all feelings of personal attachment. . . .
I know these flagging pulses of your friendship; but I understand them, and they do not separate me from you. They are
necessary to your character and are combined with other things
which I would not wish different.' What these words signify is,
no doubt, that breath of strangeness and remoteness that is part
of the destiny of genius.

Körner's critical letter disturbed Schiller. He sent it to Lotte,
as if to warn her of his faults. Her absolution should be heard:

it gives a very agreeable picture of her: 'I do not believe, dearest, that it could often happen that I should misjudge you. I, too, have often noted in you what he [Körner] speaks about, and consider those traits to be so interwoven with your being that they are an inseparable part of you; even if you had faults, I should be indulgent. It is not love if one only paints a beautiful picture in one's mind and endows it with every perfection; love is loving people as we find them, and, if they have weaknesses, accepting then with a loving heart.'

In February 1790 Karoline and Lotte travelled to Erfurt in order to see Karoline von Dacheröden, and also visited Dalberg, the Coadjutor. Schiller fetched them from there and spent a few pleasant days in the circle of friends at Erfurt. Then Karoline returned with the betrothed couple to Jena. The wedding was announced. This, too, may be described in Lotte's words, written down sixteen years after, when Schiller was no longer living: 'February 22, 1806. On a Monday, February 22, 1790, we were married in Wenigen-Jena by Deacon Schmidt. . . . We arrived in Jena on the Sunday evening. . . . On the Monday morning we three drove together to Kahla, where we collected my mother. It was a spring day, like this day in 1806 on which, with pain, I record it. We left Kahla at about two and arrived in Wenigen-Jena in complete quiet at about five; we alighted at the church; no one was present at the ceremony except my mother and Karoline. We spent the evening . . . quietly talking together over tea. Thus the day passed, which brought so much joy in its train, and so much sorrow. Everyone has his day. Mine, too, will come.'

CHAPTER VIII

JENA, ILLNESS AND A VISIT TO SWABIA (1790-94)

*

Meanwhile events had been taking place in the outside world
. . . one only needs to recount their rhythm: July 14, 1789, the
storming of the Bastille; August 4, abolition of feudal law;
August 24, the Declaration of Human Rights; October 6, Louis
XVI taken to Paris from Versailles; during the winter 1789–90,
confiscation of church property and abolition of the nobility;
the first excesses; June 20, 1791, attempted flight of the King.
There followed the invasion of the Allies, Prussia and Austria,
while in Paris there was the rule of the Commune, the storming
of the Tuileries, the September massacres and the abolition of
the monarchy. September 20, bombardment of Valmy and the
withdrawal of the Allies; January 21, 1793, the execution of the
King.

Schiller had direct information from two sources about these
events: from a Swabian school-friend who at that time was a
private tutor in France, and from Wilhelm von Wolzogen, who
was staying in Paris during the whole period of the Terror. We
know of the great hopes with which Schiller began, but we
learn, too, that even the news of the storming of the Bastille,
which he heard in Lauchstädt at the beginning of August 1789
while staying there with Karoline and Lotte, was not so joyfully
received by him as by them, but with a 'seriousness filled with
forebodings'. It was the spectacle of violence which began to
make a decisive change in his attitude towards the Revolution,
as it did in the case of Wieland, Klopstock and many other
German believers in liberty; while Goethe, of course, had

sensed earlier than any of them that the dissolution of the old, firm order must unleash forces that human hands would be unable to direct. We must once again recall Schiller's poem, *Die Künstler*, at the opening of which he set his joyful expression of confidence in his own age:

> Wie schön, o Mensch, mit deinem Palmenzweige
> Stehst du an des Jahrhunderts Neige,
> In edler stolzer Männlichkeit,
> Mit aufgeschloßnem Sinn, mit Geistesfülle,
> Voll milden Ernsts, in tatenreicher Stille,
> Der reifste Sohn der Zeit,
> Frei durch Vernunft, stark durch Gesetze,
> Durch Sanftmut groß und reich durch Schätze,
> Die lange Zeit dein Busen dir verschwieg,
> Herr der Natur, die deine Fesseln liebet,
> Die deine Kraft in tausend Kämpfen übet
> Und prangend unter dir aus der Verwildrung stieg!*

A fine, solemn-stepping proclamation of human hopes of which its author had no need to be ashamed, and which, although historical events so painfully refuted it, is not to be dismissed out of hand. Schiller's inaugural lecture at Jena, too, had still, in accord with the spirit of the Enlightenment, viewed the course of human history as an ascending path from the beginnings to the present day. Now the picture changed. While they were talking about the King's fate in Paris, Schiller seriously thought, in December 1792, of writing a memorandum in the King's defence. The matter was important enough, he remarked to Körner, to occupy the pen of a sensible man, and he was of the opinion that the French would not be insensitive to the judgment of a foreigner. And then, when the sentence had been

---

* 'How splendidly, o man, you stand with your palm-branch at the turning of the century, in noble, proud manliness, with open mind, richly-endowed spirit, filled with mild seriousness, in a stillness pregnant with deeds, time's ripest son, free by your reason, strong by your laws, great by your gentleness and rich through treasures which your bosom long concealed from you, lord of nature, which loves your bonds and tests your strength in a thousand struggles, and which, from its barbarism, rose up in splendour beneath your hand.'

carried out, he admitted: 'I cannot bear to look at a French newspaper, these butchers disgust me so' – and in the *Briefe über die ästhetische Erziehung des Menschen* (*Letters on the Aesthetic Education of Man* – 1795) the present was to be described as an age, on the one hand of relapse into barbarism, and on the other of 'laxness and depravity of character . . . the two extremes of human decadence, both united in a single epoch'. The remedy for this extreme of decadence was to be art, the service of beauty and morals; *Die Künstler* already contained the summons:

> Der Menschheit Würde ist in eure Hand gegeben,
> Bewahret sie!
> Sie sinkt mit euch! Mit euch wird sie sich heben!*

It is Schiller's exhortation to the poets. One may smile at it; one cannot extinguish its truth.

A few days after the wedding Schiller wrote to his friend in Dresden about the happiness of his family life: 'My existence has reached a state of harmonious equilibrium, not passionate and intense, but calm and bright. . . .' He had achieved that stillness of the inner life that is essential if works that will live are to be produced.

But what tasks he had to perform! First of all his lectures. In addition to the private lecture on universal history he gave a public lecture on the aesthetics of tragedy – 'in order to do something for my 200 thalers [from the Duke of Weimar]'. He gained copy from this which he could turn to cash in the periodicals. He was under contract to several publishers to edit and write introductions for collections of historical works. Again and again these introductions, in which he speaks about the Migrations, the Middle Ages and the Crusades, the Reformation and the Wars of Religion, remind one of a diviner walking across country, to whom the subterranean water must reveal its presence. Very often we are unable to accept the pre-

---

* 'Human dignity has been placed in your hands: guard it! With you it sinks, with you it will rise again!'

suppositions on which his judgments are based – and yet we are astonished at the intuitive power with which he grasps historical figures in their essential purity of outline. This is no less true of his *Geschichte des dreißigjährigen Krieges* (*History of the Thirty Years War*), after *Der Abfall der Niederlande*, his chief work as a historian. Neither of them is a scientific work in the modern sense, i.e. based on a study of sources; they are compilations from other authors' works; it is just that this compiler was a genius, who sifted other men's conclusions, investigated them and combined them to produce a convincing picture. His conception of Wallenstein in particular, begun in the historical work and completed in the drama, has been brilliantly vindicated by modern research.

To the same period belongs the plan for an epic on Frederick the Great, which Körner urged on him. For two years he carried it around with him, then he abandoned it. He wished to write the epic, not in hexameters, but in rhyming verse. 'People must be able to *sing* it!' he wrote to his friend.

For Virgil, too, of whose *Aeneid* he translated considerable passages at that time, he thought German hexameters unsuitable. He wrote it in stanzas in which, however, the rhyme is employed with a special interlacing fluidity, and succeeded in creating a German, and very Schillerian, equivalent of the 'quite peculiar magical power, the rare combination of lightness and strength' which he praises in Virgil's verse.

But this many-sided activity – history, aesthetics, poetic composition – accompanied, and justified, as always with Schiller, by philosophical reflection, can only be properly appraised if one sees it as a process, planned on a grand scale, of learn-as-you-go self-education; the late and laborious apprenticeship of a man – already a famous writer – who has seen the necessity of basing his art, in respect of craftsmanship, thought-content and what Goethe called *Weltbemerkung*,* on a sounder foundation.

In 1790 he wrote a sharp criticism of the poems of Gottfried

* Literally: 'taking note of the world'.

August Bürger.* For Schiller himself – as so often when one artist speaks about another – it was far more a matter of becoming conscious of the nature of his own activity than an attack; but Bürger was very hurt by it, and, since Schlegel† was a friend of Bürger's, Schiller's relations with Schlegel and the Romantic Movement were impaired in advance. The occasion of the review was the fact that Bürger had laid claim to the title of 'folk-poet'. The term had been coined by Herder, who had taught that true poetry must arise from the qualities peculiar to a people and a language: 'whether or not we are classical, posterity may decide'. Against this Schiller maintained that our world was no longer a unity as in olden times, when all the members of a society were close to one another in thought and feeling; today there was a great gap between the educated classes and the masses. If the claims of the former were neglected in order to fulfil the wishes of the masses, true poetry would never be attained to. So Bürger's coarse, formally slipshod folk-style was the wrong way. Higher beauty might in no wise be sacrificed to popularity. The poet, however, who succeeded in 'attuning himself to the childlike mentality of the people, without in any way compromising the dignity of art', had reached the zenith of achievement: to 'ennoble on the lips of the people' the passions as they first break forth. It is precisely this that Schiller achieves most finely in many of his later works, in others he fails to do so. But on the 'natural' path of Herder and Bürger, the path from the root to the branches, there are examples of failure. For growth, like grafting, can go wrong.

From his letters one can see how much work Schiller was setting himself just then: 'fourteen hours a day', and that for months at a time. Within four months he completed, punctually

---

* Bürger (1747–94), Professor of Aesthetics at Göttingen, was widely celebrated for his ballads and songs in the English manner, some of which, e.g. the ballad *Lenore*, became internationally known.

† August Wilhelm von Schlegel (1767–1845), with his brother Friedrich (1772–1829) one of the pioneers of the Romantic Movement in Germany, cf. 183 ff.

on the agreed date, the first part of *Der dreißigjährige Krieg*, including the collection of material and the writing, and in the autumn of 1790 his constitution began to give warning signs. On January 3, 1791, on a visit to Erfurt, he had an outbreak of 'catarrhal fever'; it appears to have been merely suppressed with violent remedies by the local doctor, rather than cured. On the homeward journey he stayed in Weimar, felt well, and had himself presented at court. Lotte remained for a time in Weimar, while he went on to Jena to resume his lectures.

Then, in the middle of January, he had a second attack, which brought him 'to death's door', as he put it. He had to summon Lotte in haste. He suffered from high fever with expectoration of blood, abdominal disorders which had to be violently purged, and great weakness. Not until a week after the fever (in those days it was always combatted with bleeding) could he leave his bed again for a few hours and 'crawl around with the aid of a stick'. In his report to Körner he mentions the persistent painfulness of a certain place on his chest and expresses doubts as to whether the illness had come to a crisis total enough to eliminate it. In Rudolstadt at the beginning of May he was attacked by 'a fearful spasm with symptoms of suffocation, so that I could not but think that my last moment had come'. He rallied once more and felt that he was on the road to recovery, 'but the following evening the attack recurred, and in a much more violent form than on the previous occasion, so that I took farewell of my loved ones and thought to pass away any minute'. Dr Starke was summoned from Jena, and all possible remedies were tried. The attacks recurred, but less violently every day, and he was soon able to get up again. 'So I am once more among the living, in case letters from Jena should have reported my death, and this last illness has reassured me as to the condition of my lungs, for despite the violent efforts I had to make in order to counter the suffocating spasms, which were so energetic that I feared I might at any moment burst a vessel in the lungs, I never once coughed blood, and strong doses of opium progressively reduced the attacks. So my fears of consumption are pretty well dispelled.' In concluding a letter to Göschen, the publisher, he excuses himself as follows: 'Such contingencies are, of course, not favourable to our calendar' (i.e. the progress on the book about the Thirty Years War). About the same time he wrote to Körner: 'All in all, this frightening attack has been very good for me spiritually. On more than one occasion during the course of it I have looked death in the face, and my courage has been strengthened thereby. In particular, I never thought I should survive the Tuesday; at any moment I thought I should succumb to the dreadful effort of drawing breath; my voice had completely deserted me, and I could only write with a trembling hand what I still wanted to say. It included a few words to yourself, which I shall now preserve as a memorial of that sad moment. My spirit was serene.' This was the courageous spirit from which his mortally stricken body was to draw for another fourteen years the strength to endure and be used as a tool for the completion of Schiller's work.

Modern medical science, using Schiller's own precise medical data, believes it can establish retrospectively the actual facts about Schiller's illness. Apparently it was pneumonia and pleurisy affecting a constitution already undermined by the intestinal infection in Mannheim and by excessive sedentary work. What remained was not consumption of the lungs, but rather a pleural abscess which, given the diagnostic presuppositions of the day, was not correctly identified and therefore could not be properly treated. The suppuration (which caused the third and severest attack) broke out through the diaphragm; the normal result of this is general blood-poisoning and death. Schiller's constitution conquered this enemy, too, but it left him with chronic peritonitis which damaged all his vital organs, and in particular impeded the proper functioning of the intestines; this led, in the summer before his death, to intestinal blockage. The result of a post-mortem dissection seems to indicate, however, that the seat of the decay was also in the lung itself, for not only were the heart chambers, liver and gallbladder in a damaged condition, but the lobe of the left lung was also totally decomposed.

During the onset of this illness, his students showed their mettle. Schiller had not merely influenced them from the rostrum, he had also been on terms of personal friendship with them, sat with them at the common table at midday, and exchanged jokes as well as serious talk with them. Precisely because he did not play the part of one in authority, and wished to train them to be, not docile pupils, but human beings with their own individuality, he became a true teacher to them, and his image in their minds became a source of blessing to them. There is much moving testimony to this fact. They must have felt that a power emanated from Schiller, such as he later summarized in the following distich:

Vor dem Tode erschrickst du? Du wünschest, unsterblich zu leben?
Leb im Ganzen! Wenn du lange dahin bist, es bleibt.*

Now that he was seriously ill, they crowded to keep watch by him. A young Balt, Karl Gotthard Grass, gives us a delightful picture of this in a letter to Lotte Schiller, in which one can detect both anxiety and tender solicitude: 'I was in Schiller's room, and . . . a picture of the suffering man and the nobility and greatness which hovered around his features and form had been deeply imprinted upon my mind. He had . . . taken some opium in order to allay the violence of the spasms, and lay there in a gentle slumber, like a marble image. You were in the next room . . . and from time to time you came to the door . . . softly in your stockinged feet, and just as softly you knelt down with folded hands before his bed. Your dark hair flowed loosely about your shoulders. . . . You had doubtless scarcely noticed that there was someone else in the room. Meanwhile the sick man opened his eyes . . . suddenly he clasped his arms passionately round your head, and remained thus resting about your

---

* 'You are afraid of death? You wish to live on without dying? Live in the whole: when you have long since departed, that will remain.'

neck whilst his strength left him again. Forgive me for daring
to describe to you a scene which . . . only immortals ought to
witness. Can you understand now, that I am unable to forget
Schiller and yourself?'

Novalis,* who was eighteen at the time, was among those
who tended Schiller. He writes – the words are an echo of a
key passage from *Die Künstler* – that Schiller was one of those
rare beings to whom the gods have revealed the lofty secret
that beauty and truth are one and the same goddess. It is necessary to revolve this superficially attractive truth in the mind
before its austerity is revealed to us. This austerity touched not
only Novalis, but later Hölderlin† as well, who, through the
agency of Schiller, became a private tutor in the household of
Frau von Kalb from 1794 to 1795, and then came to Jena, where
he lived in frequent contact with Schiller. He avers that the
latter took a 'truly paternal' interest in him; but Schiller seems
never to have recognized the genius of this greatest of his
young friends according to the laws of its own being. Hölderlin
then left Jena somewhat precipitately to return home, thence to
follow his fated path to the Gontard house in Frankfurt am
Main. We know from his own lips how Schiller 'kindled' him.
He writes: 'As long as I was with you my heart was almost too
small, and when I was away I could no longer contain it. Before
you I am like a plant that has just been put into the soil: it has
to be covered at midday. You may laugh at me; but I am
speaking the truth.' That Schiller could not only 'kindle', but
also disappoint people, is demonstrated by a young, enthusiastic
and expectant theology student who visited him – and found
him at cards with two other gentlemen, a relaxation which had
become necessary to him. He saw 'a lanky man . . . a limp

---

* Novalis (1772–1801), whose real name was Friedrich von Hardenberg,
was the leading poet of the first 'wave' of Romanticism in German literature.
His lyric poetry has a mystical fervour and a longing to transcend the world
of the everyday, whilst his novel-fragment, *Heinrich von Ofterdingen* (influenced,
as were so many Romantic novels, by Goethe's *Wilhelm Meister*), employed the
motif of the 'blue flower', symbol of the unattainable which was the goal of
Romantic longing. He died of consumption at the age of twenty-nine.

† See above, p. 35, note.

body, knees turned in, a dull eye . . . a pale, longish face without any particular expression, and in addition reddish hair and long-fingered hands twisting a handkerchief'. The visitor excused himself in confusion for having come at an inconvenient time, and fled.

Schiller had an ardent admirer in the German-Danish writer Jens Baggesen, who had visited him in Jena in 1790 and had gathered in Denmark a circle of Schiller-readers. This circle received from Jena in July 1791 the news that Schiller was dead, and observed in the poet's honour at Hellebeke in Zealand obsequies lasting three days, at which his works were read, *An die Freude* sung, and speeches made. The 'dead' man could not but be moved when he heard of it, and it was Reinhold, also a friend of Baggesen, who was the originator of a suggestion sent to Copenhagen, to the effect that Schiller should be assisted by the offer of a pension, in view of the fact that the intense labour needed to earn himself a living had made him so ill. In December a letter from Baggesen reached Schiller containing a communication signed by Prince Friedrich Christian of Holstein-Augustenburg and by a certain Count Ernst Schimmelmann, offering Schiller an annual gift of a thousand thalers for three years. 'Accept this offer, noblest of men,' says the letter, written most attractively in the accents of the age. 'Let the sight of our titles not move you to reject it. . . . You see but men before you, your brothers, not great ones who in their vanity think by such use of their riches to indulge what is but a slightly nobler form of pride.' Incidentally, this help from Denmark was of German origin. Like the Prince of Augustenburg, Count Schimmelmann, the Danish Minister, was a German (from Pomerania).

Schiller's acceptance of the gift was made in as fine a way as the manner of its offering. 'Your purpose in doing so is to promote the good; any confusion that I might feel about it would only be because you had erred in choosing the right tool to this end. But the motive which permits me to accept it justifies me in my own eyes, and allows me, even though bound by ties of the highest obligation, to appear before you with a feeling of complete freedom. It is not to you . . . but to mankind that I must discharge my debt. This is the communal altar on which you lay your gift, and I my thanks.' No man could be proud with a nobler modesty.

In the answer which he sent to Baggesen, his thanks turn into a great reckoning with his past life. 'From my mind's infancy until the moment of writing this I have wrestled with fate; and ever since I first learned to value mental freedom I was condemned to do without it. Ten years ago a hasty step cut me off from the means of existing by any other than literary activity . . . The necessity of following this profession came upon me before I was fitted for it by my knowledge and intellectual maturity. That I was conscious of this, that I did not set my ideal of a writer's duties the same narrow limits within which I was myself confined, seems to me to be a favour of Heaven, which has thus held open to me the possibility of higher progress; but the miseries of my actual circumstances were only multiplied. I viewed everything I produced as immature and far short of the ideal which lived within me; for all the possible perfection I divined, I had to hurry before the public and, myself so much in need of instruction, set myself up as men's teacher. . . . To satisfy the stern demands of art, and at the same time to gain the barest necessary support for one's literary activity, are, as I have at last realized, incompatible in our German world of letters. I have striven for ten years to combine the two, but the attempt to make it at all possible cost me my health. Interest in my activity and a few fair flowers which fate strewed in my path hid this loss from me until, at the beginning of this year, I was awakened – do you know how? – from my dream. At a time when life was beginning to reveal its full value to me, when I was close to tying a delicate and lasting bond between my intellect and my imagination, when I was girding myself for a new venture in the realm of art, death approached me. The danger did, indeed, pass, but I only awakened to new life to take up once more the struggle with fate, with reduced strength and diminished hopes. And thus the letters found me which I received from Denmark.'

There follows an explanation of what the new mental freedom which had been given to him would mean. 'I shall gain leisure-time . . . perhaps I shall regain my lost health; if not, at least mental gloom . . . will in future not lend fuel to my illness. I look into the future with serenity . . . and if my expectations of myself were but charming delusions with which my thwarted pride revenged itself on fate, I shall at least not be found lacking in tenacity and determination to justify the hopes which two excellent citizens of my century have founded on me.'

His friends from the north would have liked to have brought him to Copenhagen, but he regarded as binding his connection with the Duke of Weimar, from whom, when he fell ill, he had also received a gift of money, and he did not feel that he could just abandon his lecturer's post in Jena. Although for the present he was completely absolved from lectures, he nevertheless resumed them with a small circle during the winter of 1792 to 1793. On the advice of his doctor he had first of all sought recuperation in Karlsbad and had used the opportunity to visit the town of Eger, where Wallenstein had been murdered; for he was already toying with the plan of that great tragedy.

But it was not tragedy to which Schiller turned now that the Copenhagen pension had made possible a free choice of activity. Instead, he set about schooling himself in Kant. His still highly variable state of health, and the fact that poetry, as he says, needs the whole man with all his powers, while philosophy only requires half of him, may have had something to do with it, but it was not the primary reason for his decision. Rather, he was dominated by his consciousness, which is very obvious in the letter to Baggesen, that he must learn, must receive, before he might appear before the world once more in the rôle of giver. It was his own self-disciplined will which forbade him to give himself up to the intimations of his poetic genius before, as a thinking man, he had rendered an account to himself of the philosophical climate of his own age, as represented by Kant. Goethe, looking back in his old age, regretted his friend's years-long preoccupation with systems 'which could do nothing for him'. He was wrong. For just as Goethe could not become the poet he was without the austere labours of his scientific studies, so too it was necessary for Schiller to train himself in the use of philosophical weapons in order that, having graduated in that school and accustomed himself to wearing such heavy armour, he might then experience the free play of his own powers.

He had first become acquainted with Kant as an interpreter of human history through the treatise which Reinhold had given him. He derived the aesthetic of tragedy on which he lectured in Jena from his own practical experience as a writer. Only then did the meeting occur with the *Kritik der Urteilskraft* (*Critique of Judgment*), in the first part of which Kant develops his theory of the beautiful. The experience struck deep. It is reported that in Rudolstadt, during the critical hours of his illness, Karoline read to him those passages from the *Kritik der Urteilskraft* which treat of the immortality of the soul: 'Therefore the highest good is really only possible on the assumption that the soul is immortal, and consequently this last, being inseparably connected with the moral law, is a postulate of the pure practical reason.' There is something peculiarly moving about the thought of this man wrestling with death and finding comfort in such bare threads of dialectic, like wires stretched through an empty heaven. Schiller seems also to have continued quite satisfied with the idea that God – according to Kant's formula – was 'a permissible, indeed a justified *symbol*'. He did not feel how bare the thought was, because – as was the case with so many of his contemporaries, and above all Kant himself – it still drew nourishment from a faith which remained unconsciously in the mind and radiated warmth. This also explains at the same time why, after two more centuries during which the apostasy continued, the Kantian formula today no longer exercises the same comforting power. But then comes the most noteworthy thing, which I think most profoundly characteristic of Schiller's attitude to God: Kant conceived the beautiful, too, as being a symbol of moral good; and here, where the poet's deepest instincts are affected, Schiller objected. Beauty as a mere 'postulate of the reason' was too little for him, he *defended its reality*; he saw it, in fact, as we have already heard, as being one with truth:

Was wir als Schönheit hier empfunden,
Wird einst als Wahrheit uns entgegengehen.*

In these two lines one can clearly see that for Schiller aesthetics was the bridge to metaphysics. The outcome of the separate phases of his dispute with Kant is already indicated here and was to be propounded three years later in the *Briefe über die ästhetische Erziehung des Menschen*.

The summer of 1792 brought a reunion with the Körners in Dresden. They had had a son the previous year, Theodor Körner, the bard of liberty, who fell fighting against Napoleon as one of Lützow's volunteers.† In the autumn of 1792 the Schillers were visited in Jena by his mother and youngest sister. 'She is good,' he wrote to Körner with soberly fraternal tenderness, 'and it appears that she could turn out well.' He had only known her as a child, and now he saw her again as a fifteen-year-old girl. He found his mother 'very changed from what she was ten years ago, but after the many pains and illnesses she has endured she looks very well. I am glad to have her with me and to have the opportunity of giving pleasure to her.' The desire to see his old home again now grew very strong in him, and in the summer of 1793 Schiller and Lotte set out on their journey to Swabia.

Tending her sick husband and worrying about him had over-

---

* 'What seems to us beauty here below will one day meet us as truth.'
† Adolf Baron von Lützow (1782–1834), a Prussian officer, formed a corps of volunteers to fight Napoleon in 1813. Theodor Körner (1791–1813) was one of the many students and intellectuals who rallied to the Prussian cause, and their deeds for the liberation of their Fatherland have ever since been a German legend. Lützow's corps was almost annihilated in June 1813, and was disbanded in 1814.

4. Johann Wolfgang von Goethe.
Engraving by H. Lips

5. Duke Karl August von Weimar, a contemporary silhouette

taxed Lotte's strength, and disturbing symptoms appeared, which, however, changed to joy when it turned out that she was pregnant. Schiller saw 'the dying torch of his own life being rekindled in another'; his child must be born in his Swabian home. On August 1 the Schillers left Jena, travelled via Nuremberg first of all to Heilbronn, whence they visited his parents at The Solitude, and at the beginning of September they went on to Ludwigsburg, where a few days later Karl Friedrich Schiller was born. How his grandmother bore him proudly to the font has already been related in the opening chapter. Schiller had made only a brief announcement of his presence to the Duke of Württemberg; Karl Eugen was nearing his end and no longer considered having his now famous pupil arrested, but he was reluctant to take any notice of him. He died on October 24, 1793. The death of the 'old Herod' had no effect either upon himself or upon his family, wrote Schiller to Körner. In his successor, for good or ill, they at least had a human being to deal with. But together with Hoven, the friend of his youth whom he had found again in Ludwigsburg, Schiller visited the royal burial-vault and spoke of the man's many great qualities, which counterbalanced his faults. Anyone who spoke disparagingly of him now was not a man to be trusted.

We learn of many encounters at this time with his former friends: with the aged Jahn, with Haug and Petersen; in Tübingen, with Abel, who now occupied the chair of philosophy there (with the latter and his pupils he sat in lively conversation till late in the night). In Stuttgart Dannecker made sketches for a bust of him; with the idealizing vision characteristic of the age he hit off exactly 'the features which are dear to us'. Scharffenstein, of course, found too much calm and repose in it, and remonstrated with Dannecker: has he ever seen Schiller 'when the god within him swelled his breast and words streamed from his lips? It was too full of passion to be beautiful, moreover his voice . . . was alternately hollow and shrieking, in fact, all in all, with his red-rimmed eyes flashing fire and his disorderly, flowing mop of red hair, he looked like an apparition.'

Schiller also saw the *Karlsschule* again, and was greeted by the pupils, amongst whom his name was held in high honour, with an ovation. He listened 'graciously and with visible emotion'. Altogether, in fact, it was the young people of his homeland who afforded him the greatest pleasure, while he missed in many of his old Swabian friends the intellectual alertness of his Jena associates. But it was a Swabian who now, in the spring of 1794, offered him a most effective instrument of intellectual activity. This was the Tübingen publisher Johann Friedrich Cotta.

Cotta viewed Schiller first of all as a great political and historical journalist rather than as a poet, and wanted him as the editor of a *General European State Journal*, which Schiller seriously considered, but felt unable to trust his uncertain health. The scheme was transformed into that of a literary monthly, *Die Horen* (*The Horae*). One can see how Schiller recognized it as a means of summoning to the public forum those scattered, solitary minds in Germany which had crawled away into their shells; and we may be sure that in recruiting his contributors he had his mind on the greatest and least accessible of them, Goethe. He wrote an announcement. In it he points out the opportunity, in a very practical and convincing way, of exercising a great synthesizing influence on the contemporary German world:

'Every writer of merit has his own circle in the reading world, and even the most widely read only has a circle of somewhat greater extent. German culture has not yet reached a point at which that which pleases the best people is found in everybody's hands. But now if the nation's best writers form a literary association they thereby unite the previously divided public, and the work in which they all participate will have the whole reading world as its public.'

It was with this plan that Schiller returned to Jena in the middle of May, 1794.

CHAPTER IX

SCHILLER AND GOETHE

*

Schiller's circle of friends in Jena had been agreeably enlarged during his absence by the arrival of Wilhelm von Humboldt, who had settled there expressly on Schiller's account. A scholar of importance and later a Prussian diplomat, Wilhelm was brother of Alexander von Humboldt, the great scientist and traveller. His interests were in language and the arts. Schiller made his acquaintance through the Lengefelds and Karoline von Dacheröden, now Wilhelm's wife, and after some initial hesitation developed such confidence in him that, even before his journey to Swabia, he had invited him to come and live nearby. Humboldt confessed that he owed whatever was best in himself to their association, and he discharged his debt of thanks in what is undoubtedly the finest thing ever written about Schiller: *Schiller und der Gang seiner Geistesentwicklung* (*Schiller and the Course of his Intellectual Development*), with which, in 1830, he introduced the edition of his correspondence with his great friend. He describes there how ideas were the element in which Schiller lived. 'He never paused in continuous, automatic mental activity, which only ceased during the more violent attacks of physical indisposition. It seemed a refreshment to him rather than an exertion. This was most clearly demonstrated in conversation, for which Schiller seemed actually to have been born. He never sought for an important topic of conversation, rather, he left it to the workings of chance to throw up a subject, but from each of these he guided the conversation towards a more general viewpoint. . . . He always treated ideas as something to be produced mutually, and always seemed to need a partner in the discussion (although the latter remained conscious of merely having received the idea) and never let that partner become idle. . . . [He] did not really speak well. But his mind always strove with clarity and precision towards acquiring some new intellectual possession, whilst he controlled that striving and rose above his subject in perfect freedom. In doing so he made use of every topic with cheerful ease and it was for this reason that his conversation was always so spontaneous.'

That Humboldt, for his part, had a rare aptitude for grasping and testing thoughts and rousing to life every dormant idea, is confirmed by Schiller in a letter about him to Körner. He only enjoyed the presence of these delightful neighbours for something over a year, then the Humboldts had to move to Berlin, where Wilhelm's mother was gravely ill; they returned to Jena from November 1796 to April 1797, only to leave it then for good, but their lively discourse was continued by letter until Schiller's death.

With Fichte,* who was appointed to Jena as Reinhold's successor in 1794, a connection had already been formed on Schiller's side, and their mutual philosophical interest in Kant threw them together. Objective differences of opinion arose, which in no way affected their mutual high esteem. But Fichte, a lofty and upright man, whose *Wissenschaftslehre* (*Theory of Knowledge*) had just appeared and caught the attention of contemporary thinkers, and who subsequently, during the darkest days of Napoleonic rule in Berlin, was to utter an unforgettable

---

* Johann Gottlieb Fichte (1762–1814) was the first great disciple of Immanuel Kant (1724–1804). Accepting the Kantian theory of knowledge, he nevertheless rejected the latter's denial of the possibility of metaphysical speculation, and developed his own system of Transcendental Subjective Idealism, which views the world as a process posited by the Transcendental Ego for the advancement of its own moral progress. Fichte's philosophy fitted in with, and had a great influence on, Romantic literary theory, whilst his view that Germany had a vital rôle to play in the development of the world process led him to proclaim its mission in a series of *Addresses to the German Nation*, lectures delivered (with considerable courage) during the winter 1806–07 in a Berlin under French occupation.

call to the German nation to be mindful of its own spiritual resources, seems not to have had, like Schiller, the gift of fluent conversation which leaves one's companion his own freedom; as a result their relationship did not evolve into that easy intellectual exchange for which Schiller had hoped.

An astrologer glancing at Schiller's position on his return to Jena in that spring of 1794 would probably have cast him a dazzling horoscope: certainly one indicative of decision. If one wished to attempt a playful description of the constellation of geniuses in the Weimar-Jena firmament, one could put it perhaps as follows: Goethe's Jupiter still has Mars beside it, but in decline; Venus the bringer of peace is already rising; Fichte's Uranus, coming from afar and bound for distant places, does not disturb the others' courses. Humboldt's Mercury keeps close to the sun. Herder's Saturn, ringed round by its own loneliness, does not yet emit a hostile radiance, while from Wieland's Neptune come friendly rays.

Such was the configuration beneath which Schiller began to court Goethe's friendship. But in writing to him, on June 13, he did not approach him merely on his own behalf. 'The enclosed sheet [it was the plan for *Die Horen*] conveys the desire of a society of men who hold you in unlimited esteem to honour the periodical in question with your contributions, about whose value and quality we can have but a single voice.' Goethe's collaboration would be decisive to the success of the undertaking. Fichte was mentioned, Woltmann the historian, and Humboldt, who had all joined with Schiller in editing it; and Goethe was invited to join the committee which decided which manuscripts were to be accepted. 'The greater and closer the interest you accord our undertaking, the more will its value increase in the eyes of that section of the public whose approbation is most important to us.'

It is the letter, polite and respectful, of an editor seeking the support of a great author. But how did it look from the recipient's point of view? While Schiller had for years been preoccupied with Goethe, ceaselessly wrestling and comparing, and spurred on by his greatness as a writer, Goethe had experienced Schiller's work, not as being worthy of aesthetic attention, but as a foreign body intruding into and disturbing his domain. In Schiller's youthful works he saw 'a powerful but immature talent which has flooded our country with a full and overwhelming torrent of just those ethical and theatrical paradoxes of which I had sought to purge myself'. And *Don Carlos* had not won him over either. Certainly, he had had it performed, two years previously, on the stage of the Weimar theatre, of which he was now the director, but only after the fashion of a producer putting on celebrated novelties; after all, he was obliged to perform Kotzebue* as well. The applause with which such works were greeted, 'by wild students and educated court ladies alike', horrified one who had returned home from Italy with such totally different, hard-won aesthetic ideas. 'The manner in which I had educated myself seemed to me to be crippled and thrust aside.' In Schiller's recently published essay *Über Anmut und Würde* (*On Grace and Dignity*) he read certain 'hard passages' in which nature's favourite is warned against excessive self-esteem, and in which Schiller was no doubt thinking of his opponent Bürger, as being direct attacks on himself, Goethe. He saw Schiller as the complete Kantian filled with a sense of his own freedom and self-determination and thought him ungrateful towards Nature, which, after all, had not exactly been a stepmother to him. He declined the mediation of acquaintances, and also of the Erfurt Dalberg; agreement seemed unthinkable. And yet Schiller was a power; Goethe could not refuse his collaboration to *The Horae* if he was not, for the sake of caprice, to forfeit an important chance of exerting an influence and turning his suitor into his enemy. So he dictated a letter to his secretary, then changed his mind and wrote in his own hand: 'It will give me the greatest of pleasure to join the society.'

In July 1794 there was a meeting in Jena of the local Scientific

* August von Kotzebue (1761–1819), a prolific playwright, particularly of theatrically effective comedies which still hold the stage. He was assassinated by a student who thought he was a government spy.

Society. Goethe and Schiller were both honorary members. Perhaps Schiller had heard that Goethe would come to the meeting; perhaps it was not completely fortuitous that he took part and left at once with Goethe; we do not know, but we may safely assume the conversation that then developed to have been one of those gifts from on high for which the moment was now ripe. Late in life* Goethe recounted what had happened:

'[Schiller] seemed interested in the matter of the lecture, but remarked very intelligently and in a manner very welcome to me personally, that such a piecemeal way of dealing with nature could hardly appeal to the layman. I replied . . . that even to initiates it might perhaps remain a mystery, and that there must surely be a way of treating nature . . . not as isolated phenomena, but showing her living and acting, striving outwards from the whole to the parts. He asked for enlightenment on this point, but did not conceal his doubts; he could not admit that . . . what I had maintained could be derived from experience. We reached his house, and the conversation enticed me in; I then gave a lively rendering of *The Metamorphosis of Plants*,† and drew a symbolic plant, with many characteristic strokes of the pen, before his very eyes. He looked at and listened to everything with great interest and a sure grasp, but when I had finished he shook his head and said: That is not an experience, it is an idea. I was taken aback, and somewhat annoyed: for the point which divided us was there most strictly defined. His assertion in *Über Anmut und Würde* occurred to me again, my old anger was stirring, but I took hold of myself and replied: I am delighted to find that I have ideas without knowing it, and even see them with my eyes.'

Schiller's reply was that of a trained Kantian, to whom Goethe opposed the lively contradiction of his own 'obstinate realism', while thinking at the same time: if he holds that to be an idea which I claim as an experience, then there must be some medi-

* In his *Erste Begegnung mit Schiller*, written in old age and published with his posthumous papers.

† A poem in which Goethe expounds his idea of the organic development of plants.

ating relationship between the two. 'The first step had . . . been taken. Schiller had great powers of attraction; he held fast all who came near to him.'

Another conversation between them touching artistic matters probably took place in Humboldt's house. A few days later there arrived a letter from Weimar in which Goethe announced that he had to leave for Dessau. 'Please remember me kindly and be assured that I am very much looking forward to a more frequent exchange of ideas with you.' That was on July 25. Schiller waited. Again almost a month passed. On August 23 he learned that Goethe was back from his journey. And now he wrote the great letter – not as editor to collaborator, but as man to man.

He begins by expressing his hope of seeing him again soon. 'Our recent conversations have set the whole mass of my ideas in motion. . . . Your spiritual perception (for so I must designate the total impression of your ideas upon me) has shed an unexpected light on many things concerning which I was at odds with myself. I lacked the requisite object, the matter, of a number of speculative ideas, and you have put me on the track of it. Your observant gaze, playing upon things with such gentleness and clarity, never exposes you to the danger of following the wrong path, on to which both speculation and imagination which is obedient to nothing but itself can so easily stray. In the rightness of your intuition lies everything that analysis laboriously searches for, and in a much completer form; and only because it exists within you in its wholeness is your own treasure hidden from you; for unfortunately we are only conscious of what we analyse. Minds of your type seldom know how deeply they have penetrated, and how little cause they have to borrow from philosophy, which can but learn from them.'

It was certainly clever, in the noblest sense of the word, of Schiller to tell the other that he had need of no one to be what he already was – and at the same time to hint that nevertheless he needed him, Schiller, in order to understand himself. And indeed it meant at the same time: if you do not need me as a poet, you still need me as the man who understands you. 'For a long time I have watched, although from some distance, the course your mind has taken and the path you have marked out for yourself, with constantly renewed admiration. You seek what is necessary in nature, but you seek it by the most difficult path, one which any man of lesser powers would be careful to avoid. . . . You rise step by step from the simple organism to the more complex, to construct in the end the most complex of all, man, genetically out of materials from the whole structure of nature. . . . A great and truly heroic conception. . . . You can never have hoped that your lifetime would suffice for the attainment of such a goal, but even to have embarked upon such a course is more . . . than having completed any other – and you have chosen, like Achilles in the Iliad, between Phtia and immortality. . . .' If Goethe had been born a Greek, the bold observer continues, or even only an Italian, the idealizing tendency of his milieu would have shortened his path and perhaps made it superfluous. But as a German thrown upon this northern world of ours he either had himself to become a northern artist, or else by the power of his own thought give birth to his own Greece. 'So you had an additional labour, for just as you moved from intuition to abstraction, so now you must convert concepts back into intuitions. . . . That, more or less, is what I judge the development of your mind to have been, and you yourself will best know whether I am right. But what you will hardly know, since genius is always the profoundest mystery to itself, is the beautiful conformity of your philosophical instinct with the purest findings of speculative reason.'

And now follow the words in which he seeks to win Goethe and offers himself as his companion: 'At first sight it appears as if there could not be two greater opposites than the speculative mind which starts from unity, and the intuitive mind which starts from multiplicity. But if the first searches chastely and honestly for experience, and the other searches with free and spontaneous mental energy for law, it cannot fail to happen . . . that they should meet one another half-way. To be sure, the intuitive mind is only concerned with individuals, and the speculative mind with species. But if the intuitive mind is endowed with genius and looks for the character of necessity in empirical things, it will of course only produce individuals, but possessing the character of the species; and if the speculative mind is endowed with genius, and transcends experience without losing touch with it, of course it will only produce species, but possessing the possibility of life. But I see that I am on the point of writing a treatise instead of a letter – please forgive me and attribute it to the lively interest with which this subject has filled me; and should you not recognize your own image in this mirror, I beg you not to flee from it on that account.'

The letter was sent. Schiller, accompanied by Humboldt, travelled to Weissenfels to meet Körner; and nothing more clearly demonstrates the excitement with which he must have awaited Goethe's answer than that he said not a word to Körner about the letter and the new, closer relationship with Goethe which Körner has always so greatly desired. If it was to end in disappointment, he would put up with it himself. But he reached home, and there was the answer: 'For my birthday, which occurred this week,' wrote Goethe, 'I could have received no more agreeable present than your letter, in which with a friendly hand you sum up my existence. . . .'

The game (was it a game?) was won. And only then did he report to Körner that Goethe was at last meeting him with confidence. In his reply Goethe had expressed the wish to be acquainted by Schiller with the course of his own mental development, particularly in recent years, and Schiller complied with his request in his next letter. The intuitive working of Goethe's cast of mind, he affirmed, was the utmost any man could make of himself: 'to generalize his intuition and make his emotion a lawgiver. *My* intellect works rather in symbols, and so I am poised, a sort of hybrid, between concept and intuition . . . It is this which, particularly in my early years, has given me, in the field of speculation no less than of literature, a somewhat clumsy appearance; for usually the poet came over me when I wished to philosophize, and the philosophic mood when I wished to write poetry. . . . If I can so far master these two powers as to be able freely to delimit each, then quite a pleasant fate awaits me; unfortunately, however, after I have begun to know and use my moral powers properly, an illness threatens to undermine my physical ones. I shall scarcely have time to carry out a . . . complete mental transformation, but I will do what I can, and when the edifice finally collapses I shall perhaps have saved whatever is worth preserving from the conflagration.'

There then followed Goethe's invitation to Schiller to come and stay at his house in Weimar. It was accepted with joy, but with a request that no account should be taken of him in household matters, for his spasms prevented him from sleeping at night, so that he had to sleep during the morning; only if given complete freedom could he avoid the embarrassment of making the other dependent upon his state of health. 'Please excuse these preliminaries. . . . I only ask for the tiresome liberty of being ill in your house.'

During the two weeks which his so surprisingly come-by friend spent in his house, Goethe, whose robust and practical disposition could easily be stirred to helpful activity by the sight of a person needing such help, learned to do for Schiller what he was to practise with the most tender care for their remaining eleven years together: tending him, sparing him, gently reaccustoming him to a greater regularity in the planning of his day, enticing him out into the fresh air – for since his severe illness in 1791 Schiller had led a most unhealthy existence, working shut up in his room till all hours. The letters which enable us to observe in such detail the life they lived side by side show again and again Goethe's inventiveness in caring for Schiller: sending a fish, or beans from Christiane's garden; sending his coach in summer or his sleigh in winter; making him study Shakespeare's *Julius Caesar* to stimulate him while at work on the crowd scenes in *Wilhelm Tell*; writing to Lotte Schiller: 'Give him my regards, but without disturbing him in his work.'

Goethe gave him the freedom of the Weimar theatre, which was small and limited in its resources, but provided the dramatist with an essential visual testing-ground, so that he could now see each of his works in the process of being performed as it was written, and could study and acquire whatever devices were needful for effectiveness. Goethe became his adviser for each work, and brought into the confines of his own four walls the results of his observations of natural objects, the news of events in the outside world, even the colour of the things of which it was made up: from Goethe's descriptions of his journey to Switzerland Schiller derived the colour, atmosphere and vividness of the Swiss national character in *Wilhelm Tell*. Goethe wrote about *Wallenstein* in the *Literaturzeitung* and told the nation what it should think of the work.

On the other hand, what he received from Schiller was of no less account. 'If I have been the person who made things real to you, you in your turn have made me take a more reasonable view of the variety of man's inner life; you have given me a second youth and made me a poet again, which I thought I had almost ceased to be.' The fact of the matter is that in those years Schiller brought about the climactic in Goethe's transformation of matter into spirit, experience into idea. By inducing him to collaborate in *Die Horen* and Schiller's *Musenalmanach* (*Muses' Almanac*) he reawakened his delight in literary activity, without which many a work would have remained a mere mental project. He provided Goethe with a lasting stimulus, always ready for lively sympathy, and received the same in return. More than this human beings are scarcely able to give one another: the joy of being there for each other, for each other's advantage. On his return from the south Goethe had been lonely and misunderstood, and the coldness had touched his heart – now, at the side of a man who was his equal, for eleven years he did not need to know these things. But each had to remain what his own nature made him, and to shape his works as well as his own life out of his own substance. To strengthen each in his own individuality – that was the result

of their friendship. And this meant so much that in the spring
of 1795, after careful consideration, Schiller could only decline
a call to Tübingen, instigated by Abel, which offered him a field
of activity in his own land and favourable conditions; and he
stood by his decision when the offer was repeated.

For no shadow ever to have fallen between Goethe and
Schiller, they would have had to be superhuman. But they were
only men. A shadow on Schiller's side is perhaps a certain lack
of independence of judgment where Goethe's relationship with
Christiane Vulpius was concerned, which Goethe himself, long
before he made her his wife in the social sense, regarded as a
marriage; but Schiller's letters scarcely take any account of her,
and when they do, then not always in the happiest manner –
and Goethe felt it. But we must beware of demanding of the
people of a completely different era that extremely generous
and almost matter-of-course measure of freedom which now-
adays everyone expects for himself and his fellows. Weimar
society was united in treating a person like 'that Vulpius woman'
– who was not only common, but had also offended against
respectability – as if she did not exist. Moreover, Charlotte von
Stein had been a friend of Lotte Schiller ever since her youth,
and may well have encouraged a prejudice against the girl whom
Goethe had installed in his house as his mistress. But we know
that Schiller had for himself very definite views about the necessity for a strict code of behaviour, views which hang together
with his best virtues as a poet. His most important utterance on
this point, which does him great credit, occurs towards the end
of 1801 in a letter to Countess Schimmelmann. The latter had
renewed the old request that he should come to Copenhagen,
and had also hinted that Goethe (whom many worthy contemporaries regarded as a man of light character) was hardly the
right sort of company for Schiller. To which Schiller replied
that his acquaintanceship with Goethe had been the most beneficent event in his life – 'I do not need to say anything to you
about the man's *mind* . . . it is my profound conviction that no
other writer can even remotely compare with him in depth and

tenderness of feeling and at the same time in magnitude of artistic merit. Nature has more richly endowed him than any other man since Shakespeare. And in addition to what he has *received* from nature, he has through incessant study added more to himself than any other. In twenty years of honest effort he has slaved to study all three realms of nature, achieving a profound penetration of the respective sciences. . . . But it is not these lofty qualities of mind which bind me to him. If he did not as a man have a higher value for me than any I have ever met, I should merely admire his genius from a distance. I think I may say that in the six years I have lived with him I have not for one single moment doubted his character. There is a profound veracity and decency in his nature, and a lofty seriousness towards all that is right and proper; for that reason, gossips and hypocrites . . . have never felt comfortable in his presence. . . . I could wish,' he concludes, 'that I could vindicate [him] also in respect of his domestic affairs. . . . But, regrettably, through one or two wrong ideas about domestic happiness and through an unfortunate fear of matrimony, he has entered into a relationship which oppresses him and makes him unhappy, and which . . . he is too soft-hearted to shake off. This is his only weakness, which, however, injures no one but himself, and it, too, is connected with a very noble aspect of his character.'

On Goethe's side, what occasionally cast a shadow upon his connection with Schiller was something hidden, something that he concealed even from himself. In my view, it should not be glossed over, but squarely faced. Goethe was not able to return the profound and unreserved admiration which Schiller felt for his works, at least not in the same sense. For him, Schiller was a great and noble man, a bold and brilliant spirit – but I do not think that his friend's works, in whose production he played such a helpful and sympathetic part, represented for him a source of happiness welling up from within, such as poetry can be for the poetically sensitive man. He felt that the alloy of mind and matter in Schiller's works was the result of a conscious operation of the will, not the spontaneous product of free poetic creativity. For it is true that in Schiller the language seldom attains to a life and breath of its own, as is the case with others whom we honour as born lords of the poetic art. Schiller's language does not bewitch our senses, it gives off no fragrance. This was criticized by the Romantics, refined perfume-sniffers all, and they began to assert that he was no poet. Goethe reacted all the more violently against such a view, because he himself had once thought similarly; and it is precisely through all his many positive judgments and defences of Schiller that one sees the glint of his own suppressed objection. The criticism of Schiller which the Romantics circulated gradually gained the upper hand and conditions the image of him which is current today – or should we say rather, which was current until yesterday evening. Only it overlooked the fact that Schiller himself knew his own inadequacies better than any of his critics: 'The more sensible I become of things I lack, the firmer my conviction is of the strength of the talent which, despite my inadequacy, has brought me as far as I have already come. . . . I have shaped my own drama in accordance with my talent, a fact which ensures me a certain excellence in that field, precisely because it is my own.'

One must learn to catch the Schillerian rhythm, which is completely determined by the intellect, in order to recognize that here, despite everything, we have the great language of a great poet. As long as it is not felt as such, is not *spoken* as such on the stage, Schiller is not present in our intellectual life. It is important that we rediscover Schiller for the present day and age. And as for the 'fragrance', it is unreasonable to expect a smell of the soil from a wave of the sea.

It must have been something of this kind that Goethe, late in life and after his friend's death, began to suspect. '[Schiller's] plays are like a properly matured wine: the older they become, the more flavour they give. I make so bold as to take Schiller for a poet, and even a great one.' Which must surely mean that the greatness which he had long sensed in Schiller was also completely present in his poetic works. He called him the last nobleman among writers; and with an angry glance at the Romantic critics he remarked: 'Yes, everything else about him was proud and grand, but his eyes were gentle.' And most splendid of all – and late, in 1828 – is what Karl von Holtei has related. When he ventured to criticize Schiller's adaptation of *Egmont* for the Weimar theatre and his really very unsuitable treatment of Goethe's poetry, 'I shall never forget the glance the old man flashed at me as he said almost angrily: "What do you children know about it! Our great friend understood these things better than we do." '

However, Schiller did not live to hear these late admissions. In his personal dispute with the Romantic school, about which more will be said later, he did not find Goethe ranged decisively alongside him; instead, he took up an intermediary position. The Schlegel brothers in particular were zealous and understanding interpreters of Goethe's works – and since in Germany no poet ever has a superfluity of such persons, it is understandable that he had no wish to fall foul of them. It is also understandable, however, that this was painful to Schiller. It did not, as we have seen, make him waver in his trusting friendship for Goethe.

In his marvellous, clear, penetrating letters about Goethe's *Wilhelm Meister* he states that he counts it one of the greatest joys of his life 'that I experienced the completion of that work, that it occurred during the time of my own active striving . . . and the beautiful relationship that exists between us makes it almost a religious matter for me to make your cause my own, to develop everything that is real in me to an unblemished mirror of the spirit that inhabits this shell, and thus in a higher sense to deserve the name of your friend. How vividly have I been aware on this occasion that excellence is a force, that even on selfish spirits it can only operate as a force, and that the only liberty it permits one to take towards an excellent man is that of love.'

This insight finds poetic expression in *Das Glück* (*Good Fortune*), a poem in which he, the great fighter, offers his homage to

6. Weimar about 1805

7.   Bust of Schiller by Dannecker

the other, the man upon whom the gods have freely bestowed their blessing. Schiller calls that man happy whom the gracious gods loved even before his birth, and whom as a child Venus cradled in her arms. He says it is great, too, if one who is his own creator and shaper subdues fate by his own virtue; but such a one never wins happiness. An earnest will can preserve one from baseness, but what is highest descends as a free gift from the gods. And now the praise which overcomes itself and all pride or defiance at its own achievement:

> Zürne der Schönheit nicht, daß sie schön ist, daß sie verdienstlos,
> Wie der Lilie Kelch, prangt durch der Venus Geschenk;
> Laß sie die Glückliche sein; du schaust sie, du bist der Beglückte,
> Wie sie ohne Verdienst glänzt, so entzücket sie dich.
> Freue dich, daß die Gabe des Lieds vom Himmel herabkommt,
> Daß der Sänger dir singt, was ihn die Muse gelehrt!
> Weil der Gott ihn beseelt, so wird er dem Hörer zum Gotte,
> Weil er der Glückliche ist, kannst du der Selige sein.
> Auf dem geschäftigen Markt, da führe Themis die Waage,
> Und es messe der Lohn streng an der Mühe sich ab;
> Aber die Freude ruft nur ein Gott auf sterbliche Wangen,
> Wo kein Wunder geschieht, ist kein Beglückter zu sehn.
> Alles Menschliche muß erst werden und wachsen und reifen
> Und von Gestalt zu Gestalt führt es die bildende Zeit;
> Aber das Glückliche siehest du nicht, das Schöne nicht werden,
> Fertig von Ewigkeit her steht es vollendet vor dir.
> Jede irdische Venus entsteht, wie die erste des Himmels,
> Eine dunkle Geburt aus dem unendlichen Meer;
> Wie die erste Minerva, so tritt, mit der Aegis gerüstet,
> Aus des Donnerers Haupt jeder Gedanke des Lichts.*

* 'Do not be angry with Beauty for being beautiful, for being resplendent without any merit of her own, like a lily's chalice, through the gift of Venus; let her be the fortunate one; you see her, are gladdened by her: just as she shines without meriting it, so, too, she gladdens you. Rejoice that the gift of song comes down from Heaven, that the singer sings to you what the Muse has taught him! Because the god has inspired him, he himself becomes a god to the listener; because he is fortunate, you can be blissful. In the busy market let Themis hold the scales, and let the reward be strictly meted out according to the effort; but only a god can summon joy to mortal cheeks, and where no miracle occurs, no happy man will be seen. All that is human must suffer development and growth and ripening, and time forms it into one shape after another; but you never see what is happy, what is beautiful, developing: complete from

That is Schiller's ode to Grace, concealed in 'pagan' imagery. Grace cannot be merited by an earnest will. Because, in his humility, he knew this, he too, Herakles the hero, received the gift.

---

all eternity it stands perfect before you. Every earthly Venus arises, as did the first heavenly one, like a dark birth from the infinite ocean; like the first Minerva, every luminous thought springs ready-armed with the aegis forth from the Thunderer's head.'

CHAPTER X

POETRY, PHILOSOPHY AND DRAMA

*

Schiller's *Briefe über die ästhetische Erziehung des Menschen* (*Letters on the Aesthetic Education of Man*) crown and conclude his philosophical work and at the same time herald the period of his mature art. In September 1794 he mentions *Wallenstein* to Körner: during his stay in Swabia he had not only drawn the plan, but even sketched a few scenes; but – 'I am thoroughly frightened of this work. . . . In the truest sense of the phrase I am treading . . . a previously unattempted path; for in poetic matters I have in the last three or four years put on a completely new personality.' The aesthetic letters are the necessary foundation and vindication of this new poetic personality which he feels himself to possess, a reflection upon the nature of his task; and it is highly significant that both his philosophical and his political contemplations should thus issue in the contemplation of art. For even in the midst of his wrestlings with Kant, Schiller had had an intuition that the solution to the problems of philosophy might lie with art and the artist, and, particularly since his alliance with Goethe, he had again and again found new words to express his joyful realization that the artist is 'the only real man'. But now the *Ästhetische Briefe* attempt to unravel and heal even political life itself by means of art, 'because it is through art that men journey to freedom'. This pilgrimage of Schiller's deserves our close and admiring attention; but first his relationship to Kant, and his divergence from him, must once more be considered.

We saw that the place allotted to beauty in Kant's system

('The beautiful as a symbol of moral good') did not satisfy Schiller; the transforming effect of beauty did not receive its due from Kant. Logically, he countered Kant's categorical imperative of duty with an apt and almost Christian-sounding observation: '[Man's] pure spiritual nature has been associated with a sensual one, not in order to cast it away like a burden or slough it off like a coarse husk, but to unite it as closely as possible with his higher self.'

So far, so good. But now both poets, Goethe as well as Schiller, emptied out the Kantian baby with the bathwater by also dissenting from him when, contrary to the mood of the whole century, he taught the existence of radical evil. Of course, he was too much of a theorist to recognize evil as existing hypostatically in Satan; he made it into a principle, as he had done with God as well. For all that, it was a considerable contribution to men's knowledge of reality, that the leading philosopher of the age should have uttered a warning that radical evil existed and must be reckoned with. Goethe, however, considered that with this doctrine the great Königsberger had 'beslobbered his philosopher's mantle', and Schiller, too, rejected it as 'too monkish'. A fatal misunderstanding. For it was that which robbed Schiller's theory of the Beautiful, and the aesthetics of German Classicism as a whole, of a full validity capable of embracing the total reality of the world; and as a consequence we feel their theories today to be inadequate in many essential respects.

The *Briefe*, which were first of all addressed personally to the Prince of Holstein-Augustenburg and then adapted for *Die Horen*, are a splendid conception, equally significant in their content (educating men to be citizens and human beings) and in the clarity of their structure and the nobility of their language. They represent one of the principal achievements of Schiller's life's work and ought to be much more widely known and read. But that human nature as a whole, as Schiller thinks, had been destroyed by art (i.e. culture and civilization) and could therefore be restored by a higher art is a fundamental error in his train of thought; for human nature was damaged by sin, separation from God, and is restored by Grace, which gives back to us that lost wholeness of human nature through the incarnation of Christ and our participation in it.

I affirm the error – yet also that everything Schiller says about art as illusion and *play* is in no way affected by the error, but shines as an unassailable truth and can never be too often read, weighed and taken to heart, particularly by Germans, who are always so fond of demanding from art or reading into it things not consonant with its nature. 'Needless to say,' Schiller says in the twenty-sixth letter, 'it is aesthetic illusion I am speaking of here . . . not logical, which is confused with [truth] – which consequently is loved because it is illusion, and not because it is taken for something better. Only the first is play, since the second is mere deception. To consider the first kind of illusion of some account can never harm truth, because one never runs the risk of substituting it for the latter, which after all is the only way in which truth can be injured; to despise it is to despise all art, whose nature is illusion.' It is worth noting that it was Gottfried Benn* who in his speech at Marburg in 1951 on *Problems of the Lyric* praised Schiller's recognition of this fact. Our age does not know it yet, but it is once more very close to the insights which Schiller proclaimed. In actual fact art *is* illusion: a game relaxed in itself which brings relaxation. One can sense the smile in Schiller's words when he says: 'When dealing with the good and the perfect, man can *only* be serious . . . but he plays with beauty. . . . Man only plays when he is in the fullest sense of the word . . . human, and he is only truly human when he plays.' It is impossible to speak more 'artistically' about art. And it is all true. All the happiness that art can give is thereby defined. But when we see what has become today of the artists who play thus, and of whom Benn is one of the most consistent and honest with himself, and how dark

* Gottfried Benn (1886–1956), a modern German lyric poet who was also a hospital consultant; his poetry specializes in the clinical analysis of morbid symptoms, both medical and cultural.

with impending catastrophe is the sky beneath which their game at the crossroads is played out (punishable according to the traffic regulations, and mocked by the passers-by) – then perhaps it will not appear that I spoke from mere Christian prejudice when I stated so clearly that the notion that art is of itself capable of restoring human nature and the state was an error and an illusion. Schiller's humanist doctrine of art did not grasp the 'real presence' of the metaphysical upon earth, the participation of God and the Tempter in human history – and for that reason failed to grasp the fact that a truly free play of art is only possible when it occurs among the children of God. But we should not overlook the fact that it is precisely in Schiller's contribution to German Classical aesthetics that the memory of such sonship is very distinct: at the point where he speaks of the great age of Greece as being the youth of the human race and of poetry. Schiller still knew that man was meant to be different, was different and will again be different from what he appears today to be.

A few friends, his family, his work – it was within this inner circle that his life was concentrated. Until 1794 the Schillers lived by the market in Jena, and from 1795 onwards in the Griesbach house next to the old castle. In order to escape from his indoor existence and not always have a tiring walk when he wanted a glimpse of the countryside, he purchased in 1795 a small plot of land near the Löbder gate and built himself there a little garden-house – 'the lovely garden-terrace' as it is called in Goethe's elegy for his friend – 'from which he heard the language of the stars, which came with clarity and mystery to his equally living and eternal spirit'. In 1796 bad news about his parents reached him from Ludwigsburg, news that the French were in the land bringing an epidemic with them, and of the illness and death of his young sister Nanette and his father. His mother needed help. Schiller, himself not well enough to undertake the journey, asked his sister Christophine to do it, and paid her fare. His first son, Karl, who had been born in Ludwigsburg, was followed in 1796 by a second, Ernst, and in 1799 by a daughter, Karoline; the younger daughter, Emilie, was not born until 1804.

Whenever he needed peace and quiet for his work, Goethe would come over to Jena and spend the evening with Schiller. A friend of Körner's from Dresden, Funck, a Saxon officer, has left a description of this: '[Goethe] comes every afternoon at four o'clock and remains till after supper. Normally he walks in silently . . . takes a book, or sketches. This peaceful scene may perhaps be interrupted by the boisterous youngster, who strikes Goethe in the face with a whip, whereupon the latter springs up, tousles the boy's hair, and gives him a shaking, swears that one day he will have to thrash him or use his head for skittles, and now, without knowing how, has been set going. There follows a discussion, which often lasts till late at night . . . Schiller himself walks – one might almost say runs – around the room, he can never sit down. One can often notice his physical complaint, particularly when he is attacked by fits of suffocation. . . . If one can draw him into an interesting conversation at such time . . . his illness leaves him, only to return at once when . . . there is nothing more to discuss. . . . One can see the state of uninterrupted tension in which he lives, and how much his mind tyrannizes his body, because every slackening of mental activity produces physical illness. . . . For that very reason he is so difficult to cure, because his mind, accustomed to ceaseless activity, is continually kept tense by the illness, and because to begin a cure it would first be necessary to make him thoroughly ill. . . . If some great lord were to present him with 10,000 thalers on condition that he spent them travelling, and made me . . . his guide, who . . . was to look after his comfort, then perhaps it might be possible to help him. But with his present mode of existence he will go on working until one day, at his writing-desk, the last drop of oil is consumed, and then will go out like a lamp.'

Schiller's contact with Novalis and Hölderlin has already been mentioned. Since 1796 Schelling* and the newly-married

* Friedrich Wilhelm von Schelling (1775–1854) was another post-Kantian

Schlegels (August Wilhelm, the translator, and his wife Karoline) had been friends of the family, while Friedrich Schlegel,
the younger brother, Ludwig Tieck,* Jean Paul Richter and
later Clemens Brentano,† in so far as they visited Schiller at all,
only did so fleetingly.

August Wilhelm Schlegel had had a sort of teacher-and-pupil
relationship with Bürger, and thus was involved to a certain
extent in Schiller's criticism of Bürger. He was scarcely able to
grasp the essential nature of this dispute between two creative
personalities. Schlegel was not creative, but incomparable in
the application and development of the linguistic possibilities
created by other people; his achievement in translating Shakespeare, and transforming him into a German possession also,
cannot be overestimated. And the lectures on dramatic literature
which he later delivered in Vienna deserve to be more highly
thought of than they are. Schiller early recognized him as the
possessor of a brilliant although not profound mind, and as an
extremely useful collaborator for *Die Horen*. He sought to
recruit him, brought him to Jena and obtained a teaching post
for him at the university. Schlegel, after an initial enthusiasm
for *Don Carlos*, was critical of Schiller, and after Bürger's death
in 1794 was unwilling immediately to go over to the camp of
the latter's adversary. But for all that, he took what Schiller had
to offer, and what reflects unfavourably on him is his duplicity,
his blowing hot and cold at the same time. For while in his
letters to Schiller he regularly expressed his admiration, he

philosopher whose system (Transcendental Objective Idealism) greatly influenced the Romantic writers, with whom he had close personal contacts. The
radical pantheism of his thought later developed into a kind of pseudo-Christian
mysticism.

* Johann Ludwig Tieck (1773–1853), poet, dramatist and novelist, was one
of the founders of the Romantic Movement in Germany; he was the originator
of the *Kunstmärchen* (art-tale) form, and the principal theorist and practitioner of
the 'ironic' approach to life and literature.

† Clemens Maria Brentano (1778–1842) was one of the finest poets of German
High Romanticism. He was less of a theorist than the earlier Romantics, and
excelled as a lyric poet and writer of fairy-tales and *Novellen*. Together with
Achim von Arnim (1781–1831) he edited the most famous collection of German
folk-poetry.

managed to insinuate his own reservations into his brother Friedrich's strong and genuine admiration for Schiller. He visited Schiller's house and dined at Schiller's table, ever the respectful young man looking up to his patron, always polite, moderate, blameless – and yet at home he was writing a parody (a weak one, incidentally) of Schiller's poem *Würde der Frauen* (*The Dignity of Women*); it was not printed till fifty years later, but it passed from hand to hand in his circle. This antagonism derived in the first place from his wife, Karoline: a refined creature, and very clever. Like the Schlegel brothers, Schelling (in order to marry whom Karoline divorced August Wilhelm a few years later) was also influenced by her against Schiller. His 'high-pitched' poetic manner (as she put it) did not appeal to her, and Schiller himself soon enough detected her hostility. There is no arguing about such contrarieties, and it is not because her character was so different to Schiller's that one can reproach her but, as with August Wilhelm, for her two-faced behaviour and furtive web-spinning. Many of her letters spread hatred and scorn of him; the Romantic Movement's hostility to Schiller had its origin in Karoline's salon, and many of the judgments about Schiller which are still current sound as if even today they were whispered by her lips, not yet silenced in death.

This 'pert, cutting, one-sided manner' of the Schlegels caused him 'physical pain', wrote Schiller to Goethe. He felt this more strongly in the case of Friedrich than with the smooth August Wilhelm, and failed to see that Friedrich's was the more honest nature of the two. While the elder received acknowledgment of his achievements, the younger was treated by him in a distant and even hostile manner and thus driven all the more into the enemy's camp.

His previously excellent relations with Wieland may have been clouded for a time by the fact that the latter's *Mercury* was a vessel by means of which he could make his presence felt, whereas *Die Horen* now appeared to be taking the wind out of his sails. But Wieland was, at heart, too open a person to let this estrangement, if such it was, endure for long. Herder, however, could have added so much to the project, even by way of plain honest disagreement, and on his side there grew up year by year a sense of injury, of being no longer needed and therefore relegated to a corner; he became embittered and unfriendly.

So Goethe's alliance with Schiller and the founding of *Die Horen*, which was soon followed by that of the *Musenalmanach* (*Muses' Almanac*), instead of bringing about union, only provided, in typical German manner, a further occasion of division – man against man, camp against camp. In the first year of *Die Horen* Goethe published an essay, *Literary Sansculottism*, a sharp rejection of attacks in a Berlin periodical. And it was from Goethe, too, that the idea came of passing judgment on their opponents in the form of *Xenien* (monodistiches on the pattern of Martial's *Xenia*). Schiller took up the idea with enthusiasm and invented a sort of dramatic plot for them: the *Xenien* are frivolous fellows travelling to market, heedless of the excise-officer who wants to delay them, and setting up their stall:

Martial
Xenien nennet ihr euch? Ihr gebt euch für Küchenpräsente?
Ißt man denn, mit Vergunst, spanischen Pfeffer bei euch?

Xenien
Nicht doch! Aber es schwächten die vielen wäßrigten Speisen
So den Magen, daß jetzt Pfeffer und Wermut nur hilft.*

The salutary intent of the erstwhile regimental surgeon is thus neatly defined. A large part of the *Xenien*, so it has been reported, were composed by the two friends jointly during the early months of the year 1796. 'If one turned out well, its success was signalled by a burst of immoderate laughter, which

* *Martial*
You call yourselves Xenia? You say you are kitchen-gifts?*
By your leave, do they eat cayenne pepper where you come from?
* Xenia = guest-gifts.
Xenia
Not so. But so many watery dishes have weakened the stomach to such an extent that now only pepper and wormwood are any use.

penetrated the ceiling to reach Griesbach's ears.' (Griesbach was the professor, Schiller's landlord, who lived above him.)

In the autumn of 1796 appeared *The Muses' Almanac for* 1797; it opened with serious poetry: *Alexis und Dora* by Goethe, and by Schiller *Die Klage der Ceres* (*Ceres' Lament*), the fine *Votivtafeln* (*Votive Inscriptions*), which belong to his most powerful poetic utterances, and other works – and to round it off the *Xenien* as a poetic epilogue. It caused a great stir; the first edition was soon sold out and was followed by a second and a third. One cannot blame those who were the target (including the Schlegels) for failing to enjoy the joke and show a proper appreciation of the greatness of artistic viewpoint in this playful didactic poem; but the rejoinders which appeared were so pitiful that Schiller was right when he said: 'If there is anyone who still cannot see that the *Xenien* are a work of poetry, he is past help. Coarseness and offence could not have been more thoroughly distilled off from wit and humour.' Neither Goethe nor Schiller produced a counter-reply. But when Friedrich Schlegel reviewed first *The Muses' Almanac* and then the most recent pieces in *Die Horen* in his mocking way, Schiller also showed his brother and Karoline the door. One can see that he did it with a sigh of relief: 'Within the circle of my close acquaintances there must be a feeling of complete security and unlimited trust, and that, after what has happened, can no longer be the case with our relationship.' Not even Goethe could persuade him to reopen his house to the Schlegels. The only consequence of the latter's mediation was that a complete break was avoided, and the brothers were induced not to attack Schiller again publicly, but as men well-versed in the trade of letters they had more than enough devices and connections at their disposal for diverting their opinions into other channels, or observing a damaging silence where he was concerned – and they missed no opportunity of doing Schiller whatever harm they could by these means. A painful consequence of the quarrel was that the young poetess Sophie Mereau, whom Schiller had advised in the composition of her early efforts, and whose wit and charm had, in all innocence, touched his heart, was lost to him when, by her marriage to Clemens Brentano, she found her way into the Romantic camp.

Thus Schiller, who after years of pedagogical and philosophical activity was just returning to creative writing, found himself, with his new, mature type of work, facing criticism which was partly uncomprehending and partly consciously hostile. It is only because the new works were so effective in sweeping aside all obstacles that we are unable in retrospect to grasp properly what it meant for him to issue a challenge to the whole literary world, as he had done in the *Xenien*. He risked more by it than Goethe, whose most difficult poetic productions were being praised and interpreted by the young Romantics; Schiller really possessed that splendid courage of which his friend said that it 'sooner or later conquers the resistance of an obtuse world'.

The poems and ballads he produced between 1795 and the *Almanac for 1800*, which contained *Das Lied von der Glocke* (*The Song of the Bell*), would have needed, not prejudice ever ready to mock, but a particularly sensitive and strictly discriminating ear, if they were to be justly appreciated. In his treatise *Über naïve und sentimentalische Dichtung* (*On Naïve and Sentimental Poetry*) Schiller had himself laid down the best guide to such an appreciation. His new mode of poetic utterance had outgrown the violence and unevenness which frequently disfigured his youthful poems, but there are still only a few isolated pieces [e.g. *Erwartung* (*Expectation*)] which may be classed as lyrics in the narrower sense. His versification, whenever it attempts to express emotion, is often clumsy: it was easy for the Schlegels to make fun of it. Schiller's language only comes into its own when it is able to give expression to a process, not of feeling, but of thought; then, even in rhetorical passages, it becomes supple, unerring in its loftier flights; then he has the gift of producing authentic imagery, not imagery imprinted upon the material as if with a pastry-form, e.g. in *Das Reich der Schatten* (*The Kingdom of the Shades*), *Das Glück* (*Good Fortune*), *Der*

Spaziergang (*The Walk*), *Sänger der Vorwelt* (*Singers of Antiquity*),
Nänie (*Threnody*), *Das Eleusische Fest* (*The Eleusinian Festival*) –
or in the parable-like narrative pieces *Die Teilung der Erde* (*The
Division of the Earth*) and *Pegasus im Joch* (*Yoked Pegasus*), which
form a transition to the subsequent ballad-poetry.

'When you receive this,' he wrote to Humboldt, to whom he
sent his recently-finished *Das Reich der Schatten,* 'put away everything profane and read the poem in dedicated silence.' What he
here demands of the reader (who would dare to do so today?)
is in fact essential to its understanding; one must be prepared to
accompany the eagle in its flight, not just watch from one's
armchair. Schiller's great poems will regain their full effect
when people are once more able and willing to meet them with
that elevation of spirit which the poet can then develop, inten-
sify and heighten:

> Froh des neuen ungewohnten Schwebens
> Fließt er aufwärts, und des Erdenlebens
> Schweres Traumbild sinkt und sinkt und sinkt . . .*

This conclusion of *Das Reich der Schatten* describes the elevation
of the great man of action, Herakles, to the thrones of the gods.
Schiller dreamed of a sequel, an idyll in which Herakles would
be shown on Olympus. 'If I were to succeed in this undertaking,' he confesses, once more to Humboldt, 'then I imagine
I should have triumphed by means of sentimental poetry even
over naïve poetry itself.† . . . Just think . . . a poetic representation in which everything that is mortal has been extin-
guished, nothing but light, perfect freedom, pure potentiality.
. . . I really feel dizzy at the thought of the task and the possibility of its solution. . . . I am not in complete despair at it, if
only my mind can be completely free and washed clean of all

---

* 'Rejoicing in this strange, new hovering feeling, he floats upwards, and
earthly life with its oppressive dream-vision sinks and sinks and sinks. . . .'

† In his essay *On Naïve and Sentimental Poetry* Schiller distinguishes, with an
eye on Goethe and himself, the poet in whom poetry is a spontaneous product
of feeling immediately expressed ('naive' poetry) from the one in whom it is
the result of reflection ('sentimental' poetry).

the dross of mundane life; I will then concentrate my entire strength and the whole of the ethereal part of my nature for one more great effort, even if I should expend myself completely in the act.' One might think this quite remarkably modern, ·almost an anticipation of abstract art. But if that is not what is meant, at least it betrays the longing which Pascal put in Christian terms when he said that God meant man to be 'greater than himself', a longing which one could apply to Schiller's thought somewhat as follows: poetry must become greater than itself if it is to perfect itself.

Viewed from this standpoint, what happens in the ballads is a return to the world. In the dispute with Bürger, we have already touched on the point which makes it difficult for us to appreciate the Schillerian ballad: it does not, like the ballad of Herder, Bürger, Goethe and their successors, follow the natural course from root to branches – it does the reverse. Sometimes it fails. *Der Eisenhammer* (*Ironhammer*), *Der Drachenkampf* (*The Dragon-fight*), *Hero und Leander* – such ballads, one cannot avoid the conclusion, are school-exercises in the application of a preconceived stylistic concept, rather than poems. But when the difficult operation succeeds, we have works for which the word 'ballad' is perhaps an inadequate label, but which are simply masterpieces *sui generis*, an indispensable part of our poetic heritage – *Der Taucher* (*The Diver*), *Der Handschuh* (*The Glove*), *Das Ring des Polykrates* (*The Ring of Polykrates*), *Die Kraniche des Ibykus* (*The Cranes of Ibykus*), *Die Bürgschaft* (*The Pledge*) – right up to the last, *Der Graf von Habsburg* (*The Count of Habsburg*), which interprets the imperial office in its sacramental sense and makes the singer its herald.

Das Lied von der Glocke (*The Song of the Bell*) is also a masterpiece *sui generis*, and while its weaknesses – the occasional lapses into banality of expression – are so obvious taken by themselves, the grandeur of the total effect is irresistible. It cannot be better described than in Humboldt's words: 'I know of no other poem in any language which in . . . such a small compass releases such a wide range of poetry, runs the whole gamut of profound sentiment and . . . shows the most important epochs and events in life as if enclosed within the natural bounds of an epic.' It is this, namely – and not just a paean of the German middle classes – that is the essence of the poem, which depicts its author's unique mission so marvellously in the image of the bell, when he makes it swing aloft high above the lowly life of earth, 'the neighbour of the thunder', the voice of heaven, like the stars

> Die ihren Schöpfer wandelnd loben
> Und führen das bekränzte Jahr.
> Nur ewigen und ernsten Dingen
> Sei ihr metallner Mund geweiht,
> Und stündlich mit den schnellen Schwingen
> Berühr im Fluge sie die Zeit.*

One need not envy critics whose conception of lyric poetry can find no room for such a paean as this.

Finally, the lyric poems of the last years in Weimar, produced for social occasions or theatrical requirements, like the riddles for *Turandot* and the songs for *Wilhelm Tell*, are often the inspirations of a relaxed and more terrestrially-inclined moment – whose favours are celebrated in a particularly fine example – and have a surface glitter which has misled many an observer into underestimating their poetic content. To this group belong the cheerful *Punschlied* (*Punch Song*) and also the serious poem *Thekla: Eine Geisterstimme* (*Thekla: a Phantom Voice*), with its remarkable harp-note transparency.

For years all Schiller's work had been produced in the shadow of the most urgent and difficult of all his tasks: *Wallenstein*. It had been begun in 1793, hesitantly reconsidered in 1794, seriously tackled in 1796. From now on his letters give us a detailed description of the protracted toil, often interrupted by illness or other work, which it cost the poet to master material that was 'intractable in the highest degree'. 'But it had to be just

* Which praise their Creator in their courses and lead the garlanded year. Let its metal mouth be consecrated to none but serious and eternal things, and hourly let time touch it with swift wings in its flight.'

such a material,' he wrote to Körner, 'with which I could open my new life as a dramatist. Here, where I am walking on a knife-edge, where every sidestep could mean destruction for the whole . . . where I can only reach my goal . . . through truth, necessity and constancy, the decisive crisis of my poetic character must ensue. . . . I am purposely seeking for limitation in the historical sources, in order that my ideas may be strictly determined and realized by surrounding circumstances . . . they must be *animated* by that force which I have already been able to show where necessary, and without which any thought of this undertaking . . . would have been absolutely impossible.' Verse proved to be the indispensable artistic instrument of this animation; originally, although he had employed it so felicitously in *Don Carlos*, he had intended to dispense with verse, but had recourse to it again and found himself under a 'totally different dispensation'. But verse increased the size of the play; it had to be divided up, and grew into a trilogy.

The Prelude, *Wallensteins Lager* (*Wallenstein's Camp*), was first performed on October 12, 1798, in the newly-constructed theatre in Weimar. The Prologue, written by Schiller for the occasion, solemnly proclaimed the duty of the art of drama to treat of 'the great themes of humanity'. We easily forget that for Schiller the Thirty Years War was no further back than the age of Schiller, Goethe and Napoleon is for us. It was recent history, whose themes and shocks still reverberated, however much the face of the world and the climate of opinion had changed.

Most of us, in Germany at any rate, make our first acquaintance with the subject, Wallenstein's rise, his treachery towards the Emperor and his fall, in the artistic version of it given by Schiller, and so we usually never realize what a feat of composition he achieved, with what admirable power the wide-ranging, divergent events are compressed into the compass of a terse and firmly-articulated plot: the fall of the princely man and his house. It was a stroke of genius to set the great general's *camp* before our eyes – if it had been depicted during the action itself, it would have impeded it at every point. ('For it is his power which leads his heart astray / His camp alone can explain his crime.') And what a piece it is! The poet of whom people are fond of saying that he was only able to create ideal types, not human beings, is here seen at the height of his skill as a delineator of character. The soldiery are depicted in all their types: the sergeant-major, a Wallenstein in miniature ('The very way he hems and spits / Has faithfully been copied by you'); the confident Pappenheim cavalry; the wild men from Holk's Horse Rifles; the faithful Tiefenbach arquebusiers. And there are superb characters like the sutler-woman and the Capuchin. All this is not just genre-painting, but fitted into an action which, like a river, grows from many little tributaries and aims at the heart of the tragedy, its irresistible momentum rising from speech to song with 'Come then, comrades, to horse! to horse!' Has anyone, except perhaps Uhland,* written a finer soldier's song? No wonder the camp-song of Wallenstein's soldiers fought in the War of Liberation against Napoleon, a sound as of a waving banner at the head of the warrior hordes.

And now to the structure of the tragedy itself, which it is absolutely necessary to consider as a unity, for which reason it would also be necessary, if the work is to have its full effect, for it to be performed in a single day. For the trajectory of the action reaches from the beginning of *Die Piccolomini* (*The Piccolomini*) to the end of *Wallensteins Tod* (*The Death of Wallenstein*), it rises, culminates and falls. It is a single process.†

The exposition is masterly: Wallenstein's position between the generals and the soldiers who still adhere blindly to him, and the Court of Vienna (represented by Questenberg) which fears him. And as a sub-plot the position of Max Piccolomini between his commander, whom he reveres and whose daughter he loves, and the bonds uniting him with his father, his duty and

---

* Ludwig Uhland (1787–1862), German lyric and dramatic poet, author of songs, ballads and romances in a popular style which were highly prized in their day.

† See synopsis, pp. 200-1.

the Imperial House. The circumstances and the characters, what is to be hoped for and what feared, all this is presented in such a way that it can be taken in at a glance, that one cannot fail to understand it. The action rises till the moment when Wallenstein, compelled by his stars and the pressure of outside circumstances (i.e. the exposure of his treasonable plans through the interception of his go-between), takes the decisive step towards an alliance with his country's Swedish enemies. What was later to appear in *Demetrius* as the real tragic problem of power already flashes out here in Wallenstein's great monologue, a metaphysical light playing upon the game of high politics: the moment when he becomes conscious that his betrayal of the Imperial Power strikes at the root of 'the pious, childlike faith of the peoples'.

The spiritual climax is represented by the conversation between the imperious commander, already overshadowed by the dark cloud of his own destiny, and the youthful Max Piccolomini, who has had such a fervent faith in him, trusted in his purity of purpose, and now sees him plunging into guilt. The scene is among the finest in world literature. (I am often amazed, when listening to the conversation of friends, to find how little it is known.) For here, namely, the mentalities (or, rather, the predicaments) of the politically entangled and the morally absolutist man confront one another, not just rhetorically, but empirically as creature to creature. They touch, and then separate – tragically, hopelessly. I do not know how anyone who is at all sensitive to the spectacle of human conflicts issuing in the shape of dramatic action and speech can watch with anything but the deepest emotion the messengers, the riders bearing Wallenstein's decision to the enemy, hastening down the long road. An iambic line of more than pentameter length renders the picture unforgettably:

> Es ist zu spät. Indes du deine Worte
> Verlierst, wird schon ein Meilenzeiger nach dem anderen
> Zurückgelegt von meinen Eilenden,
> Die mein Gebot nach Prag und Eger tragen.

– Ergib dich drein. Wir handeln, wie wir müssen,
So laß uns das Notwendige mit Würde,
Mit festem Schritte tun. Was tu ich Schlimmres,
Als jener Cäsar tat, des Name noch
Bis heut das Höchste in der Welt benennet?
Er führte wider Rom die Legionen,
Die Rom ihm zur Beschützung anvertraut.
Warf er das Schwert von sich, er war verloren,
Wie ich es wär, wenn ich entwaffnete.
Ich spüre was in mir von seinem Geist.
Gib mir sein Glück, das andre will ich tragen.*

From this point onwards the action plunges 'like water hurled
from crag to crag'.† The attempt to implicate the army in its
commander's treachery fails. Wallenstein finds himself stripped
of his power, surrounded only by a few of his partisans. The
act of Max Piccolomini in tearing himself away from his commander with his troop of Pappenheim cuirassiers and leading
them to their death has often been regarded (I have done it
myself in the past) as theatrically effective but lacking in inner
justification. I no longer view it in this light. Schiller knew as
well as we do that both as a human being and as an officer Max
had no right to play thus with his men's lives; but he shows
here, even more convincingly than in the cases of similarly-
placed characters like Ferdinand and Luise Miller, or Posa and
Don Carlos, how an idealistic philosophy of life, under the
pressure of empirical circumstances, is drawn as if blinded into
a vortex in which it sinks and perishes. Young Piccolomini is
not held up as a model: he falls as a victim. 'That is the fate of
beauty in this world'; this line, put into the mouth of the serious

---

* 'It is too late. While you are wasting words, my hurrying messengers are
leaving behind milestone after milestone as they bear my command to Prague
and Eger. – Resign yourself to it. We act as we must, so let us do what is necessary with dignity and a firm tread. Am I doing anything worse than Caesar,
whose name is to this day applied to what is highest in the world? He led against
Rome the legions which Rome entrusted to him for her protection. When he
cast his sword away, he was lost, as I should be if I disarmed. I feel something
of his spirit within me. Give me his luck, the rest I will bear.
† In Hölderlin's poem *Hyperion's Song of Fate* human life is compared in its
transience and suffering to 'water hurled from crag to crag'.

young girl Thekla, is an almost frightening revelation of the tragic view of life to which the author of the *Briefe über die ästhetische Erziehung des Menschen* had here attained. Now he can really no longer be accused of an inadequate perception of reality. That is what always happens: a genuine poetic gift will always grasp reality with unconscious root-fibres that probe deeper than any theory.

A heavy sky and a dim light lie over the last conversations Wallenstein has with those near to him: reflective, lingering, everything *ritardando*, while one can feel the weight of impending disaster bearing in from outside, and one knows Wallenstein's murderers are already waiting in the background. It is then that the spirit makes a place for itself in the heart of an event from political history; we hold our breath, and sense that it is not threatened kingdoms and the fall of the mighty, but what goes on in a human soul, that is the real content of the story. Schiller aimed with conscious artistry at this contrast between unrest in the outer and calm in the inner circle, as can be seen from a passage in a letter to Goethe of October 2, 1797: 'It will greatly heighten the tragic effect,' he said. And truly, it does.

Urged on by Iffland, who wanted it for Berlin, and Goethe, who was waiting to put it on in Weimar, Schiller completed the work. On January 30, 1799, the birthday of the Duchess Luise, *Die Piccolomini* was first performed on the stage, and *Wallensteins Tod* had its première on April 20. In the winter and again during the spring Schiller went to Weimar to conduct rehearsals with Goethe. The work was highly successful, and its success was repeated in Berlin and then on one stage after another. The great age of German drama had dawned.

CHAPTER XI

THE LAST PLAYS

*

The picture of Schiller in his last years is that of a cathedral-builder who has pitched his tent on the site, determined not to yield from the spot until the cathedral is finished or its builder's life has been consumed. Already, in the spring of 1798, he had given up *Die Horen*, and *The Muses' Almanac* for 1800, which appeared in the autumn of 1799, was the last he edited. He wished to devote his poetic powers, which had matured during this long period of training, entirely to the drama. A few days after the last part of *Wallenstein* had been performed on the Weimar stage he wrote to Goethe, from Jena again, that he was busy with the plan of a new tragedy, *Maria Stuart* (*Mary Stuart*); he had toyed with the idea years ago in Bauerbach, and now, immediately after the immense labour of *Wallenstein*, he began work upon it. He knew that death was at his back, a silent pursuer casting a shadow over his shoulder, and his heart could find no rest except in restless activity.

During this work he realized that it had become necessary for him to live in Weimar within sight of the theatre. In September 1799 Duke Karl August granted an increase of salary to meet the higher cost of living in the residency. In October his daughter Karoline was born, and now the move to Weimar was to take place, but instead of recovering from her confinement Lotte contracted a nerve-fever, and Schiller wore himself out nursing her, with the worry and nightly vigils. But when his wife was better at last, and the family had moved to Weimar early in the winter, his own illness recurred. 'This winter,' he says in a letter to Cotta the publisher, 'will long remain in our memory, I fear.'

Not until April was he able to resume his interrupted work on *Maria Stuart*. He had not remained idle during that difficult winter, however, and had newly translated and adapted *Macbeth* for the Weimar stage – very drastically, it must be said, turning Shakespeare's saga of the north into a piece of Weimar Classicism. It goes without saying that the Romantics took it very amiss; but the mixture of styles has that personal charm which, for example, the Baroque sometimes achieves in transforming Gothic churches.

In May and June 1800, in the forest peace of Schloss Ettersburg, the fifth act of *Maria Stuart* was written, while in Weimar the parts for the first four acts had already been allocated and rehearsals were under way. The first performance took place on June 14; reports state that its success was even more immediate and decisive than that of *Wallenstein*. From the point of view of dramatic craftsmanship, Schiller achieves complete mastery here. The action is constructed with all the author's old innate sureness of touch, but it no longer serves, as in his revolutionary youthful dramas, to document a state of mind intent on overthrowing the world as it stands. Instead, the process begun in *Don Carlos* now reaches fruition in *Wallenstein* and *Maria Stuart*: we see the historical figures in their own peculiar tragic necessity, and the sight of them arouses in the spectator's mind that catharsis which is a purifying feeling of life and thus, of course, still tends – working from the depths, from the centre, as it were – towards a salutary refashioning of the world. Schiller expressly observed that he did not intend his Mary to arouse a sentimental mood: 'the pathos must be a profound general emotion rather than a . . . feeling of individual sympathy'. Nor did he intend to prejudice the spectator against the royal hypocrite, Elizabeth of England. Instead, he paints a picture of the two queens as he had of Philip of Spain, Wallenstein and Octavio Piccolomini: bold, free and true in a broad historical sense; and it is this profounder rightness, perhaps only accessible to the eye of the poet, which, while by no means cancelling out moral judgment, certainly puts it in its proper perspective, for what we experience here is the reality of the political event. In doing so, as is well known, Schiller departed from the facts as they stand in the history books: there was no Mortimer, no love of Lord Leicester for Mary, no confession and absolution for the condemned woman; and while the poet confronts a twenty-five-year-old Mary with a thirty-year-old Elizabeth, in fact, at the time of her execution, after nineteen years of captivity, she was forty-five, and Elizabeth fifty-four; above all, there was never any personal meeting between the two queens. On the stage of world history, however, they stood face to face. And so, for the poet, tragic truth demanded that these two should be made to meet upon his stage; this is the climax towards which the action of the drama hastens, only to turn, after the fulfilment of her hope, to Mary's ruin.

Such liberties (as also those in *Wallenstein* and the much greater ones in *Don Carlos*) left untouched the real nature of the course of historical events. It is doubtful whether the same can be said for Schiller's treatment of *Die Jungfrau von Orleans* (*The Maid of Orleans*). The appearance of Joan of Arc in the spring of 1429, of which the immediate consequence was the saving of France from the hands of her English enemies, can only be conceived of as miraculous by even the most sober-minded person; miraculous, namely, in that it actually brought about a change of heart which revived the courage of the defeated and broke the courage of the conquerors. Even Joan's captivity and her death at the stake as a witch in 1431 could not nullify this effect. Our present-day feeling is that it is precisely for the severity of its events that history should be understood as a manifestation of the Divine Will operating through it, and so we must affirm that its profounder meaning had been distorted here by Schiller when he turns the life of the young saint into a gaily beribboned fairy-tale about the age of chivalry, which ends with Joan's glorious death on the battlefield, draped in banners. We cannot accept that, we feel that it is a falsification of a

167

harsher but greater truth; and, above all, Schiller failed to capture the touching, childlike quality of the historical figure when he allowed his heroic maiden to indulge in torrents of splendid high-flown theatrical rhetoric. We feel more at ease with a representation like those given by Shaw and more recently by Mell in their plays about Joan; and of the latter I really believe that, not only historically, but artistically as well, it is to be preferred to all other treatments of the subject.

But it is possible that opinion about *Die Jungfrau von Orleans*, which is Schiller's most difficult play from our point of view, may once more take a turn in his favour, as indeed, having been begun in 1800 immediately after the completion of *Maria Stuart*, and finished in the spring of 1801, the play became the greatest theatrical success Schiller ever had. It took not a little courage at that time, when Voltaire's satirical poem *La Pucelle* was still in everyone's mind, to treat the subject at all in a serious way. Schiller's work was first performed, not in Weimar, but in Leipzig, in his presence, and the public – according to an eye-witness report – 'received the author as no one had ever been received, not even a prince, to my knowledge'. At the end of the play the pit gave him three cheers; the students formed a double lane outside and told one another to keep quiet when the poet came out; heads were bared, and in silence they allowed the tall, stooping figure with the open features etched by suffering to pass through the crowd. What had aroused such deep feelings of gratitude and pleasure in these people was the victory of courage in Joan the Maid over all the opposition and mis-understanding of the rest of the world. In just such a manner the Baroque painters had represented Michael the Dragon-slayer as a dancer triumphing with supreme ease over the fire-breathing Worm; and the ease of this victory, too, pointing to the absolute mastery of the angel over the demon, is an aspect of truth. In Schiller's written discussions with Goethe there occurs as early as December 1797 the important passage in which he expresses his conviction that it was necessary 'to produce the light and air in which art may flourish by eliminating the mere common imitation of nature, and this can best be done through the introduction of symbolic aids which, in everything which does not belong to the real world of the poet's art and thus should not be depicted but merely signified, will take the place of the object concerned. I have not yet been able to develop properly this idea of symbolism in poetry, but there seems to me to be a good deal in it. If its correct use could be determined, the natural consequence would certainly be a purifying of poetry, a growth of concentration and significance in its own domain, and a correspondingly greater effectiveness within those limits.' All of which seems to prove that in *Die Jungfrau von Orleans* he was consciously aiming at a new, unrestricted dramatic form transcending historical realism; he would have accounted for the banners covering the body of Joan, instead of a witch's hat and the stake, as being 'symbolic aids', which means that Thomas Mann's observation was very much to the point when he called the play a 'word-opera'.

His efforts to achieve a form heightened to the pitch of poetic symbolism did not cease with *The Maid*. Even before tackling *Wallenstein* Schiller had been carrying around with him the plan for a drama to be called *Die Malteser* (*The Knights of Malta*): the situation of the Order during the Turkish siege. He had put the scenario on paper, jotted down thoughts about it and sketched individual scenes. Of all the plans in Schiller's important dramatic sketch-book, this was the one which occupied him most continuously and which cropped up again after each completed work, to be thought over and short-listed once more. He wished to write it on the model of Greek tragedy, with choruses. The great advantage of the subject was the simple and self-contained nature of the plot. 'Not only is the Order an entity completely *sui generis*, but at the moment of the tragic action it is even more so,' he writes. 'All communication with the outside world has been cut off by the blockade, the Order is forced to concentrate upon its own self, upon concern for its own existence, and only the qualities which made it the Order it is will be able to preserve it in this moment.' But in May 1801 he confessed to Körner that he still needed 'that dramatic event towards which the action hastens, and through which it is resolved'. Since *Die Malteser* was a subject which could not provide him with this *punctum saliens*, Schiller took the astonishing course of producing for himself, as if in a retort, a subject of the sort he needed, in which there was 'a growth of concentration and significance in the domain of poetry itself'. This was *Die Braut von Messina* (*The Bride of Messina*).

We are accustomed to seeing Schiller laying hold of his projects in the way a carpenter grasps a piece of wood, to fashion them according to his will and needs. We know that his friend's hasty way of going about things, this habit of commanding the Muses, as it were, was sometimes a source of surprise and concern to Goethe, who was so totally different in his treatment of his subjects, cautiously waiting, listening for sounds of growth. And now Schiller proposed to 'make' a subject! The thought would never have entered Goethe's head. Poets have flourished in many climes, but certainly none other would ever have attempted anything so intrinsically impossible – or, like Schiller, have been able to carry it out.

Who will deny that the plot of *Die Braut von Messina* is a farrago of incredible nonsense? The ruler of an imaginary Kingdom of Sicily receives from an oracle an evil prophecy concerning his youngest child, Beatrice: if she grows up she will become a fire-brand that will consume her brothers and destroy her father's house. He orders her death, but her mother saves her with the help of an aged servant. The King dies, the girl grows up, and her two brothers, who have only just been reconciled through the efforts of their mother, both have to fall in love with Beatrice, not knowing that she is their sister, and to destroy one another in their quarrel. The story was invented on the analogy of the old Oedipus legend and similar themes; but, of course, it cannot help but lack the mythical soil from which such old fables derive their mystery and their actual truth. What Schiller gives is a concoction, a completely artificial product; but such is the energy with which his mind can turn thoughts into speech and an invention into a theatrical plot that it is not only made possible, but compelling and convincing. The air of history blows across his invented Sicilian kingdom; Queen Isabella before the Elders, the two semi-choruses of the hostile brothers, the great reconciliation scene with the mother and the two sons, and finally the tragic conclusion contrived with such artifice: all these have luminosity, dramatic power and human dignity. Goethe, who looked on in amazement and saw the impossible succeeding, considered that the ground of the theatre had been consecrated to a higher purpose by this manifestation. The impression made on the younger section of the audience at the first Weimar performance was so strong that they cheered the poet, a thing they had never permitted themselves previously at that courtly shrine of the arts. Schiller wrote to Iffland that in this work he had tried to compete with the writers of ancient tragedy, and in doing so he had thought more about himself than about the public; he was convinced, however, that a mere dozen of such pieces would suffice to bring about the acceptance of the genre; but for all that he would leave it at the one attempt for the time being, 'since one man on his own just isn't sufficient to wage war on the whole world'.

That was two years after the completion of *Die Jungfrau*, in the spring of 1803. In the meantime, through the good offices of Duke Karl August with the Emperor, Schiller had been raised to the nobility. It was mainly an affair of Weimar society, for, as Schiller explained to Körner, 'it was somewhat strange that, of two sisters, the one [Karoline, as the wife of the Lord High Steward von Wolzogen] should have held a high place at court, whilst the other [Lotte] should have had no access to it. . . . For me, of course, it represents no great gain.' More important was the fact that Schiller had been able to acquire his own house in Weimar. On the day they moved in, April 29, 1802, his mother had died in Cleversulzbach. The son had sensed her approaching death, and was unable, when he learned of the coincidence of the dates, to shake off a feeling of gloomy foreboding. His illness was his daily companion, he was familiar with it and had come to terms with it, and during the times when he could not trust himself to make the greater effort involved in his own creative work, it had become his habit to employ his pen in some lighter task such as adapting or translating someone else's play for the Weimar stage; in this way the adaptation of Gozzi's *Turandot* was made in 1801, in the spring of 1803 that of two comedies by Picard, and as late as 1805 the translation of Racine's *Phèdre*. These were subsidiary works, during which his mind was occupied with the great labours of his own tragic art, tirelessly scheming, wrestling, testing.

He knew nothing about his most powerful rival, young Kleist, who, during those same months in the spring of 1803 in which the closing scenes of *Die Braut von Messina* were being written, had been Wieland's guest at Osmanstädt, his property close to Weimar. He, too, was striving to snatch the laurels of the old tragedians with his tragedy *Robert Guiscard*. The cordiality and understanding with which Wieland received the young poet is well known, how he tried to overcome his shyness and induced him to give a reading of the play he had begun, and how deeply impressed he then was by it, seeing in Kleist the perfecter of the tragedy of Aeschylus, Sophocles and Shakespeare, born 'to fill the great gap which, in my opinion at least, not even Schiller and Goethe have yet filled'. It goes without saying that it is only a daydream when we devise conjunctions for the poets in their courses and try to imagine what, so united, they would have been able to achieve. And yet it is less easy to abandon the dream when we see them so near to each other in space and time and striving towards the same goal – and then when we have to read in a letter written by Schiller in the spring of 1803 to Humboldt, who was staying in Rome at the time, that 'poetry as a whole is in a lamentable state at the moment', and that there could be no thought of holding together for some valuable purpose; 'each one stands alone and has to defend his own skin as if he were in the natural state'. One would like to behave as children do in a garden, who love to dig a channel with hand or hoe between one watercourse and another – and inevitably one would then recognize that nothing can be done to assist or divert a river on its lonely way to the ocean; and also that an alliance of minds such as took place between Goethe and Schiller is one of the most rare and unrepeatable gifts of fate.

From his most difficult experiment, *Die Jungfrau von Orleans*, Schiller turned to the simplest of all, the folk-play – and was now obliged to learn from practical experience what he had already known and expressed when, in 1790, he wrote his review of Bürger's poems, namely, that nothing is so difficult as what is utterly simple, and that a truly popular style, 'so far from making the poet's work easier . . . , in fact adds one difficulty more and, to be sure, [is] such a difficult task that its successful accomplishment may be termed the highest triumph of genius. What an undertaking, to satisfy the queasy taste of the connoisseur without thereby becoming unpalatable to the mass of the people!' It was just this that Schiller achieved in *Wilhelm Tell*. The 'queasy' – i.e. extremely fastidious – taste of the connoisseur must, however, really be fastidious and discriminating to appreciate properly the mastery which is at work here – while any truly simple mind can make the play its own without more ado. It is amazing with what sureness of touch the loose bundle of epic events is gathered into a unity, and how from scene to scene only what is essential, and nothing but what is essential, is presented. The man who wrote it had never been to Switzerland; and even though he had Goethe as his friend, who told him about it, he still had to be Schiller in order to reproduce it as he did: the aboriginal world of the heroic idyll, alp and mountain lake, dawn over the timber forest, and the Swiss people with their lives and feelings, all depicted with convincing truth and power. As soon as one can shake off one's prejudice about knowing *Wilhelm Tell* all too well from one's school days, so that it seems a mass of quotations and platitudes, as soon as one is able to see it with fresh eyes, then there is no end to one's admiration.

It is remarkable how Schiller came by the subject, in fact almost had it thrust upon him. For when, during the nineties, Goethe planned an epic on the subject of Tell, only to abandon it, Schiller was still far from recognizing that it was to be *his* subject. It was necessary first of all for an unfounded rumour to circulate to the effect that he was working on a play about Tell, whereupon he took notice, read the histories of Switzerland by Tschudi and Johannes von Müller – and was amazed at his find. To be sure, he called it a 'devilish piece of work'; but 'if the gods are kind to me and let me carry out what I have in my head, it will be a mighty work which will shake the theatres of Germany'. He had been engaged in preparatory work since 1802, and in the summer of 1803, after the completion of *Die Braut von Messina*, he promised Iffland that he should have *Wilhelm Tell* for the Berlin theatre 'before the winter is over'. While he was at work on it Madame de Staël appeared in Weimar, a woman of great intellectual gifts and overflowing eloquence, a French emigrée and opponent of Napoleon who had a great influence on European public opinion. She wished to make the acquaintance of the Weimar celebrities; she interviewed them, so to speak, in the name of the world-spirit. Goethe and Schiller were certainly very great writers, but for all that the subjects of a German pocket-principality. So there was nothing for it, although they had better things to do, but to talk to Madame de Staël in French (for of course she had no German) about philosophy and literature, God and creation. The efforts they made on her account were worthwhile, for without these conversations in Weimar her book *De l'Allemagne* would probably not have turned out in such a way as to inaugurate later in France a new attention to and understanding of things German. But Schiller, when, after a lengthy stay, the lady finally departed, complained of feeling as if he had endured a serious illness. For all that, *Tell* was safely completed on February 18, 1804, and performed forthwith in Weimar, Berlin and elsewhere with the greatest success. The poet's expectation that he would shake the theatres of

Germany was to be fulfilled beyond his wildest dreams.

For Napoleon, whose ever-growing power was a threat to the liberty of all nations, Schiller – unlike Goethe – had no admiration at all, and it is worth noting what he objected to about him: 'This character is completely repugnant to me – *one never hears a single cheerful remark from him.*' In the opinion of Karoline von Wolzogen, it was not in Schiller's nature to submit to any power that was not exercised with wisdom and moderation. But his opposition was based on humanitarian, not national grounds; he expressly stated that it was mean and petty to write only for a single nation. His attitude towards his own nation may be seen in the outline for a centenary poem, *Deutsche Größe (German Greatness)*, which was sketched in 1797 but not executed:

'May the German,' it reads, 'at this moment, when he is emerging without glory from a lamentable war, when two arrogant nations have set their foot upon his neck and the victor decides his fate – may he be aware of himself? May he boast of his name and take pride in it? May he lift up his head and with self-respect take his place in the ranks of the nations?'

'Yes,' comes the answer, 'he may! He has emerged unhappy from the struggle, but that in which his true value consists, that he has not lost. . . . Even if the Empire were to perish, German dignity would be unimpeached. It is moral greatness, it resides in the culture and character of the nation, which is independent of its political fate. . . . That which is shaped and ruled by spirit must itself finally be granted rule . . . and the slowest nation will catch up with the fast and fleeting ones. Then the other nations will have been the flower that falls. When the flower has fallen, the golden fruit remains, takes shape, swells to the harvest. The precious possession of the German language . . . when we look in this mirror . . . an admirable picture of ourselves meets us. We can express the youthfulness of Greece and the idealism of the present day. No capital and no court exercises its tyranny over German taste. . . . We have as many individual growths and varieties as we have provinces and rivers and customs. The lap of corruption, the mercenary courts of kings, have not equipped the German with a cheerless philosophy of self-seeking, a cheerless materialism. . . . His wise men are not orators. Therefore, for him the sacred has remained sacred. The world-spirit has singled him out to work at the everlasting task of building human culture during the struggles of the age. . . . Everything of value that other ages and nations have produced . . . has been preserved by him, is not lost to him, the treasure of centuries. His not to shine in the moment and to act out a part, but to gain the whole process of time. In the course of history every nation has its day, but the German's day is the harvest of the whole of time.'

We can see that Schiller's humane thought is not without an element of proud confidence in German nature and its mission. But now, in showing Germans in his *Wilhelm Tell* a national rising on behalf of freedom and justice – which was certainly not done without the intention of offering them spiritual consolation – he does not depict the struggle in all the division and gloom which are its normal concomitants in this troubled world; nor in the way Kleist, a few years after *Wilhelm Tell*, would show such a rising in his *Hermannsschlacht*,* in which the saviour of his country, solitary and scheming, everlastingly plotting stratagems, struggles against foreign domination and the lethargy and cowardly treachery of his own people. Schiller did not do that. He showed it in an elevated and ennobled form, softened by its heightened idealism.

This is good and fine and admirable; it is not the only thing art is capable of, but it is a lofty and indispensable potentiality. Yet we must not seek to conceal the point at which such a transfiguration departs from the truth. It is the same danger-point in Schiller's thought which we have already recognized – the 'enlightened', idealistic view, namely, that knows nothing of radical evil and Original Sin and therefore expects that the

---

* In *Die Hermannsschlacht* (*The Battle of Arminius*, 1808) Kleist (cf. 42, note) used the story of the defeat of Varus by the Cheruscan chieftain in A.D. 9 in order to express his hatred of Napoleon and the French and his disappointment in the German and Austrian rulers of his day.

human sum can be done without leaving a remainder; reason and morality would gradually accomplish everything, and a legitimate demand like that of an oppressed nation for its freedom could be enforced without flaw or blemish here below. Because Schiller believed that, because he wanted to prove it, he made his simple man of the people, Tell, deliver a lengthy monologue before his murder of Gessler on the hollow road near Küssnacht, made him reason, tried to bring him into the light by confronting him with Johann the Parricide,* the murderer from ambition. Such reasoning is false; and this represents the limits of Schiller's insight, as of any purely human morality. For there are no reasons in heaven or earth which will *justify* a murder, no reasons which give a murderer the right to say: 'I lift clean hands to Heaven' . . . as Tell does to the Parricide. He ought not to face the people and let himself be fêted; concealment and solitude would be fitting for him. Nothing can lead a man out of the darkness of an act of homicide, even if it was necessary and inevitable, but the recognition and admission of guilt, and the forgiveness which comes through the experience of Grace.

* An historical figure, Duke John of Swabia.

CHAPTER XII

BERLIN, *DEMETRIUS* AND LAST ILLNESS

*

In the spring of 1804 Schiller seriously thought of leaving Weimar. To his brother-in-law, Wilhelm von Wolzogen, he wrote in March: 'I like it less here every day, and I am not willing to die in Weimar.' A court living in a village – for that was the real state of affairs in Weimar – certainly had its charms and advantages, but it is understandable that a man like Schiller must sometimes have found it stifling. He had already complained in a letter to Humboldt of 1803 about the 'accursed stagnation' of conditions in Weimar, and even about Goethe, because the latter was 'letting his maundering habits gain the upper hand. If Goethe still had faith in the possibility of achieving something good, and was consistent in his actions, a good deal could still be accomplished here.' At the time, Schiller was probably as little aware as anyone else in Weimar that there had been a quarrel on Fichte's account, whose daring philosophy was regarded by Duke Karl August as being tantamount to a 'danger to the State', between Goethe and his sovereign, and that Goethe had been obliged to accept a sharp reprimand for his defence of Fichte. The latter had been peremptorily suspended from his duties at Jena and had gone to Berlin. His leaving had the effect of drawing others after him; almost overnight, Jena, till then the most active and sought-after university, found itself deserted by many of its most important teaching-staff: Woltmann, Hufeland, Loder, Schütz and Schlegel took posts in Prussia, while Schelling and Paulus went to Würzburg. In addition, the emigration to Halle of the *Literaturzeitung* could not be prevented, and the loss was only offset, thanks to the swift intervention of Goethe, by immediately starting a new *Jena Literary Journal*.

On May 1, 1804, we suddenly find Schiller in Berlin, together with Lotte and his two sons. He announced his presence to Iffland from the Hôtel de Russie, Unter den Linden: 'I had travelled to Leipzig on business, and it occurred to me there that I was ten leagues nearer to Berlin . . . and so I resolved on the spur of the moment to make a trip here. So here I am now, dear friend, filled with a sincere desire to greet you and my other friends; I feel the need of a new, larger element, I am looking forward to . . . widening my field of vision. I am completely exhausted from the journey, which I undertook somewhat too hastily, and shall be unable to stir from the spot today. But tomorrow, when I have recovered, kindly permit me to present to you your faithful old friend Schiller.'

This, coming from the pen of such a great idealist, is an exceedingly diplomatic document. It had only occurred to him in Leipzig that he was ten leagues nearer Berlin? He had decided on the spur of the moment to make the journey? But he hints at the same time at what he wants Iffland to notice and help him to procure: Schiller 'feels the need of a larger element' and wants to 'widen his field of vision'. That surely means: you can have me in Berlin if you want to. And then he forthwith effaces the impression left by his intention – for nobody shall say of him that he offered himself – by underlining once more the haste of his journey. All this can only be read with amusement and admiration, since it reveals once more the political streak – in the highest sense – which ran through this bold character. For that poets are mere unworldly fools is nothing but an amiable favourite delusion of the public and a cosy dream of the powers that be. We recall that even his clever school-friend Scharffenstein thought that, had Schiller not become a great poet, he could have become a great figure in public life; and it was Wilhelm Grimm* who said of him: 'When Schiller gains a

* The younger of the brothers (Jacob Grimm 1785–1863, Wilhelm Grimm

kingdom, he has had it in his mind from the beginning.'

Berlin gave the poet a brilliant reception. In his honour, Iffland had *Die Braut von Messina, Die Jungfrau* and *Wallensteins Tod* performed at his theatre, and when the guest appeared in his box the audience rose and acclaimed him. He met Fichte and his other old friends from Jena, as well as Unger, the publisher of *Die Braut von Messina*, and the musician Zelter. He was invited to dine with Prince Louis Ferdinand, and on May 13 he had an audience with Queen Luise, during which he also saw the young Prince Wilhelm, who sixty-seven years later was to be the first ruler of the Bismarck Empire. Nothing definite is known about the actual course of the negotiations with Schiller; it appears that the crafty Berliners had to draw out his wife on many topics on which he thought fit to remain silent. On May 17 he saw Privy Councillor Beyme in Potsdam, where he was offered a permanent salaried post at the Academy in Berlin and also, doubtless, employment as history tutor to the Crown Prince Friedrich Wilhelm. It is an idle and yet quite exciting day-dream to imagine Schiller to oneself as the gardener in the nursery of the Prussian future. Schiller was invited to state his terms, and the royal couple then invited him again to breakfast at Sanssouci; such were his prospects when he left for Weimar on May 18, arriving again on the twenty-first. Lotte, who did not wish to influence his decision, did not let him notice the great joy it was to her to see the wooded hills of Weimar once more, and that she did not like the idea of being transplanted to the large capital city.

With this possibility in view, however, Schiller now saw in a much clearer light what he already possessed in Weimar. We may assume that Goethe, when he learned of the Berlin scheme, begged his friend to remain at his side. Goethe had been unable to prevent the cream of Jena University from leaving, and Herder, life with whom had not been easy in his latter years, had died in December 1803. Neither Goethe nor Schiller could

---

1786–1859), scholars famous for their philological works and their collections of Germanic myths and fairy-tales.

deceive himself as to what Germany and Weimar had lost in him. Were they themselves now also to abandon their late and happy alliance? It must have been very moving for the younger man if now he really heard the older, whose friendship he had had to seek for so long, asking him not to leave him. We do not need to know more precisely what occurred. Suffice it to say that Schiller addressed himself to Karl August in a frank and sincere letter, which is clever in its very frankness, and put the Berlin offer before him:

'It could never occur to me to accept any position without your most gracious consent. . . . I know what I owe to Your Highness's favour, and I do not believe myself to be one of those mercenary fellows who dissolve the most sacred bonds from . . . mere avarice. Not only the obligation of gratitude, but also inclination and the bonds of friendship chain me to Weimar. The prospect of a dazzling situation would never, therefore, lead me into temptation. But, gracious Sir, I have a family, and although I have a perfect sufficiency with what Your Highness's generosity has granted me annually and with what I earn by my own work, I have still been unable to put away much for my children . . . my health is weak, and I must think of the future. . . . My life here is so expensive that I will gladly continue to contribute two-thirds [of my literary earnings] if through Your Highness's generosity I am put in a position to lay aside a third . . . for my children.'

The Duke consented that his salary should be doubled, with the prospect of a further increase at a future date; he was also willing to allow Schiller to visit Berlin from time to time in order to see his plays performed, which might perhaps procure a good pension from there as well; 'I hit upon this idea in order to recompense Schiller for his upright behaviour by offering him a means of improving his position still further . . . and in order to have a little game with the Berliners.' On June 18, in a letter to Beyme, Schiller rejected the proposal for a complete move to Berlin, but declared himself ready to reside there for several months each year. No reply to the offer came from

Berlin. It may be that the affair was merely delayed in its passage
through the usual official channels, or – as seems probable from
Friedrich Wilhelm III's subsequent attitude to the moving
spirits of the Wars of Liberation – that the performance of
Wilhelm Tell which had meanwhile been loudly applauded by
the Berliners had inspired misgivings in the King about a poet
who sang of freedom in such all-too-compelling accents. For
Friedrich Wilhelm had them all at his disposal: Stein,* Fichte,
Kleist, Gneisenau,† Scharnhorst,† Clausewitz;‡ but he never
gave them scope for the full exercise of their talents.

Meanwhile, Schiller's illness, which had seemed for a time to
be lurking in the background, once again made its presence felt
and interrupted any plans of a far-reaching nature. About the
middle of July 1804 Schiller went with his family to Jena, for
Lotte wished to await the birth of their fourth child there under
the care of Dr Starke, whom she knew well. On the day before
Emilie was safely delivered, Schiller suffered a severe attack:
'Such a violent colic that Starke believed he was past help, and
feared an inflammation of the bowels.' The last phase had set
in: damage to the bowel operation led to a stoppage, and it is
sad to have to read that a man so inured to pain could not
suppress the cry: 'I can endure it no longer, if only it were all
over!' Convalescence was more difficult than it had ever been
since the first severe attack in 1791, and not until October was
he able to write to Körner that hopes of recovery were returning, 'which for eight weeks I had almost abandoned. I also feel
the ability and the inclination for activity'.

Schiller's active prudence, his evenings and nights spent in
wrestling with his poetic mission, the patience, to which all
bear witness, with which he endured the years of misery caused

---

* Karl Freiherr von und zum Stein (1757–1831), a Prussian statesman celebrated for his reforms, who prepared the ground for the liberation of his country
from the French.

† Neithardt von Gneisenau (1760–1831), a Prussian general responsible,
together with Gerhard von Scharnhorst (1765–1813), for the reform and re-
habilitation of the enervated Prussian army during the Napoleonic era.

‡ Karl von Clausewitz (1780–1831), a Prussian general, was Gneisenau's
chief of staff and a famous writer on military tactics and the theory of war.

by his illness – all these nevertheless do not make up the sum total of his being; one must also take account of the unaffected cheerfulness and childlike enjoyment of life with his family and friends, if one is to understand him properly. Exemplary conduct in the hour of danger, 'but of such a light and cheerful kind that no one can reproach you with it': Schiller applied to himself this demand which Prince Eugene* the Noble Knight addressed to his officers, and he fulfilled it. In the description of the Leipzig painter Schnorr von Carolsfeld we can see how he approached a guest: 'I found [Schiller] with his little daughter Karoline in his arms, her head resting against his cheek and her arms clasped around his neck, walking, almost dancing, around the twilit room. He came towards me like this, greeted me in the friendliest manner possible, and stopped. "Now, Karoline," said the happy father, "shake hands with the gentleman, he is a good man." The child gave me a searching sidelong glance from her great blue eyes, and then slowly offered me her hand, without, incidentally, changing her position.' In the description of Heinrich Voss, the son of the man who translated Homer, we also read of him as a tender father who played with his children and 'rolled on the floor' with them. Voss assisted Schiller as a copyist during the last winter before his death. 'I shall never forget,' he says, 'the intensity of the gaze which sometimes rested upon his last-born, Emilie . . . as if he could never exhaust the happiness he found in her possession.' Voss writes very tellingly about the 'serious laughter which toned down his majestic physiognomy and saved it from too great an earnestness.' . . . 'You cannot believe,' he writes in amazement, 'and simply cannot grasp how amiable the man was.' And Karoline, his clever sister-in-law, recorded: 'I never saw that faint expression round the mouth and cheek which betrays the struggle of mockery with good-nature more charmingly imprinted upon a human countenance . . . [but] joy at other

---

*Prince Eugene of Savoy (1663-1736), a famous Austrian statesman and general. He repelled the invasion of the Ottoman Turks, and was Marlborough's ally in several of the latter's famous battles against the French.

people's faults and delight at one's own sharpness in detecting them were for him an indication of a low nature. Amusement at what is ridiculous should fly like a dithyramb through the conversation, he said. He never let the line be crossed which divides mockery from malice and teasing from gloating.'

His love of cheerfulness and his noble sense of moderation seem to me to be most happily hit off in this description. Goethe's *Epilog*, of course, also praises him as an 'easy companion' and 'one who was always ready for cheerful exchanges'; but at the same time there was always about him the air of one from on high, an angelic quality. Many felt that.

He had scarcely recovered from his serious attack before he began work on his last great play, which he was not to finish: *Demetrius*. He had long been occupied with a similar subject from English history. 'In England in the reign of Henry VII,' we read in his notes about it, 'an imposter, Warbeck, arose, who gave himself out to be one of the sons of Edward IV whom Richard III had had murdered in the Tower. He was able to offer an ostensible explanation of his escape, he found a party willing to recognize him . . . a princess of the House of York . . . knew about and supported the imposture, in fact she was primarily responsible for setting Warbeck on the stage. After he . . . had played his part for a time, the enterprise misfired, he was defeated, unmasked and executed.' This Warbeck tragedy was now abandoned by Schiller for that of the pretender Demetrius who, at the beginning of the seventeenth century, was successful in claiming and gaining the crown of the Russian Czars, forcing Boris Godunov from the throne, but was then recognized for an imposter and came to a violent end. There were also external factors which partly determined this choice of a Russian theme. Karoline's husband, his friend and brother-in-law Wolzogen, had conducted negotiations in St Petersburg as the emissary of the Weimar court and had brought about the marriage of Karl Friedrich, the Crown Prince of Weimar, with the Russian Grand Duchess Maria Pavlovna; so Schiller had reason to anticipate that a drama on a subject drawn from

Russian history would be viewed with particular interest by the ruling houses of Weimar and Russia. At the same time the subject, in its Russian setting, acquired a note of strangeness and grandeur, sensuousness and magnificence, 'the completely new quality of the subject, which has never before been seen on the stage'; but the decisive factor for Schiller was that he could make his Russian pretender believe at first that he was *really* the Czarevitch. Only thus could a human tragedy be made out of an imposture based upon a concept rather far removed from our present way of thinking, the legitimacy of princely blood. Fully and freely believing in his rights and his mission, young Demetrius appears before the Polish Diet at Cracow in order to beg for Poland's help in his expedition against Godunov. A powerful opening scene. There is an inner connection with another scene which was conceived as the climax and turning-point of the play, but which only exists as a sketch: where Demetrius, in possession of power and of the crown after his victory over Godunov, finds himself face to face with the man who, as he believes, protected him and saved him from his pursuers – and from whose lips he now has to hear that he deceived him, and with him the whole world, that he *made* him a prince: 'I gave you what you could never hope for, what birth does not give you. The whole world, and you yourself, think you are Ivan's son. You are not Ivan's son! Your birth gives you no right to this crown.' With these words he has destroyed the mainspring of Demetrius's existence, his consciousness of being in the right; an 'immense change,' notes Schiller, 'takes place in him, his silence is terrible, and is accompanied by a frightening expression'. He interrogates the man to find out if anyone beside him knows the secret. The man reassures him: all the accessories are dead. And now, when the other, having done him the greatest injury possible, demands his reward as kingmaker, he strikes him down. The man was the murderer, commissioned by Godunov, of the real Demetrius, so he has got his deserts; but the pretender, alone now with his bitter knowledge, is no longer the pure man he was a few minutes

before, he has blood on his hands and his heart bears the mark
of his knowledge that power on earth cannot be gained without
guilt, that it only comes with violence and deceit. 'You have
pierced the core of my existence,' Schiller makes Demetrius say,
in his sketch of the scene, to the man he has killed, 'you have
robbed me of my faith in myself! I am an enemy of men. The
truth and I have parted for ever! What? Shall I myself snatch
the people from their error? . . . I must go forward, and yet I
can no longer do it from my own inner conviction. Blood and
murder must maintain me in my place.' Immediately afterwards
– and this, too, exists only in sketch form – he has to confront
the Czarina Marfa, who hopes to find in him the son she lost
and who has been restored to her, but she at once feels that he,
the pretender, is not that son.

'The moment,' notes Schiller, 'is one of the greatest tragic
situations.' And it really is. One may doubt whether Schiller
himself was aware of its metaphysical profundity, for he too
was involved in that obscuring of the power of transcendental
perception which the Enlightenment brought in its train. But
in one sense Schiller achieved more than mere perception: he
invented and created the situation. For this is more than just
an exciting scene in a story about princes, a mere political event.
It becomes nothing more nor less than a symbol of human
destiny, of man himself, who, after the Fall, no longer enjoyed
the free possession of justice and happiness proper to the newly-
created human being, but instead, having been forced to recognize the devastation of sin in his nature, suddenly awakens to
the truth and cries: it is not I, I am not the son, even my mother
no longer knows me. I have no right to the crown.

It may be objected that this is interpreting Schiller's work in
a more Christian sense than is consistent with the poet's own
philosophy of life. But to raise this objection is to overlook the
fact that the 'child of the house' is one of Schiller's main themes.
It is implied in nearly every one of his great works, one of the
posthumous dramatic plans actually bears that title, his great
reflective lyric poetry is always pondering the sonship which

man lost and must regain, and the idea also plays a vital part in his philosophy, even though he anticipated that the winning-back would come through art, not faith, as we have seen in the *Briefe über die ästhetische Erziehung des Menschen*. And now, in the sketches for *Demetrius*, Schiller depicts in all its seriousness the historical situation of man when he is not reconciled through Christ with the Father, but is at the mercy of the world and its guilt. His insight into the stern truth of history, as revealed in these sketches, is deeper than in any other of his works to date. The tendency to palliate, which still dominated the historical image in *Wilhelm Tell*, has been overcome here. The hard, naked rock of human history is exposed. But that is the foundation upon which we must build, in the humility of our knowledge, our earthly habitation.

The entry of the Grand Duchess Maria Pavlovṅa, the young Crown Princess of Weimar, was due to be celebrated in November 1804. Both court and town prepared for her reception, but the theatre had nothing new ready for the festivity, and in Schiller's report to Körner one can read how Goethe, shortly before her arrival, was suddenly overcome with the fear 'that he alone had done nothing about it . . . and since he strained his inventiveness in vain, I was finally obliged to come to his aid with my own. So in four days I composed a little prelude which was straight away learnt off and performed on the 12th of November. It was successful beyond all my expectations, and I might have striven for months without managing to produce anything as acceptable to the whole audience as was this fleeting little work.' This was *Die Huldigung der Künste* (*The Homage of the Arts*), in which Schiller once more expressed the content of his aesthetic theory – the arts as the begetters and educators of 'real life' – in clear, soaring, free-flowing verse. The court, the people, the Crown Princess herself listened with emotion to the lovely act of homage. But there was a dark background to the festival. Of course, no one was aware of how close the ancient Holy Empire of the Germans already was to its fall. In 1806, under the hammer-blows of Napoleon, it would crumble. But a presentiment of the powerful shocks that would change the world had long been felt; and a note of melancholy and of farewell echoes through this greeting of the arts devised by a doomed poet.

At the festivities, 'during which one can never spare oneself', Schiller caught a severe catarrh. 'My health is unfortunately so weak that I must immediately pay for every carefree pleasure with weeks of suffering. And so, with the best will in the world, I cannot prevent my activities coming to a halt as well.' It was a hard winter. Instead of getting on with *Demetrius* he again had to find a lighter occupation, the already-mentioned adaptation of Racine's *Phèdre*, which was performed on January 30, 1805, for the birthday of the Duchess Luise. A fresh attack occurred on February 9; in a letter of February 22 he now admits that he knows his health to be 'shaken to the roots'. About the same time Goethe was also seriously ill with renal colic. As soon as Schiller was able to go out again, he visited him in his room, and young Voss, who was present, tells of the friends' reunion and the silent emotion of their embrace. Even during this last period Schiller's letters to Goethe show him alertly sympathetic, seizing every opportunity of stimulating the productivity of his often hermit-like and secluded partner and keeping it in motion through his penetrating understanding. In March he himself gradually regained his strength, and at once turned again to the great work he had begun. 'I have fastened myself on my work with all my powers. . . . It was difficult, after so many breaks and unfortunate episodes, to take up my position again, and I had to force myself to do it. But now I am in full flow.'

When we know to what an extent creative activity engages and exhausts a poet's whole being, and when we see Schiller wrestling during these last weeks before the end with the darkly realistic visions of his *Demetrius* tragedy, then it is peculiarly moving to read in the notes made by those near to him that he requested 'fairy-tales and tales of chivalry' as reading-matter; 'it is there that we find the material for everything that is great and good'. Freedom had always been the concern of his lofty spirit, not merely in the political sense, and not just the ethical concept of freedom; he was concerned (as Eduard Spranger has formulated this vital insight) 'quite simply with the fact that the soul demands another world than that which experience gives it, and that the imagination with fierce energy . . . builds worlds beyond the constricting reality it is familiar with'. This is that dream of an idyll about Herakles' elevation to Olympus which Schiller once mentioned to Humboldt: 'nothing but light, perfect freedom, pure potentiality'; he had wanted to concentrate 'the whole of the ethereal part of his nature' on it, even if he should completely expend himself in doing so. Fate decreed otherwise. His strength was to be consumed in a work that demanded from him a very austere picture of the state of the world. Once more one seems to glimpse the angel wrestling with the weight of his earthly task.

On April 28 Schiller went to the court, and on the evening of the 29th to the theatre. Goethe, who had called on him, did not feel well enough to accompany him, 'and so we parted outside his front door, never to see each other again'. When Heinrich Voss visited Schiller the next day, he found him in a fever. His condition rapidly grew worse. 'His eyes were sunk deep in his head, and every nerve twitched convulsively.' It was hard for him to take farewell of his children; he did so with tears. But when asked how he was, he replied: 'Better, brighter all the time.' His servant, who watched by him at night, heard him talk much of *Demetrius* in his fever; then, he said, he called on God to preserve him from a lingering death. And Karoline relates: 'On the last morning of his life [May 9] he pulled himself up, looked nobly up to heaven as if he had summoned all his strength, and said several times: "Judex".'

With this invocation of his Judge his course reached completion. The pains and the burden of his task were lifted, 'and this earthly life / With its oppressive dream-vision sinks and sinks and sinks'. His last act was a smile of thanks for Lotte, who 'lifted his head on to a more comfortable side'. Towards midday he fell asleep. Karoline and Lotte, who were waiting in the next room, took hope. But then they were called in. 'Something like an electric shock passed over his features, then his head fell back and utter peace transfigured his countenance.'

Goethe, who was himself too ill to be told straightaway of his friend's death, and who also did not attend the very quiet night funeral, gave no immediate expression to his grief, in fact he was unable for weeks to visit the family; so much the purer were the words of sorrow, praise and comfort he found for his song, the *Epilog zu Schillers Glocke* (*Epilogue to Schiller's Bell*).

EPILOGUE

*

A hundred, or even two hundred years, are but a short span in the course of history. It is strange to think that they could suffice to change the attitude of a nation to one of its greatest sons as radically as the attitude of Germans towards Schiller seems to have changed today. The young people who lived with and after him had hardly a single question of urgent concern to which they did not find an answer in him. Cast off the fear of earthly things, overcome the resistance of the dull world, and if you do not stake your life, you will never conquer life! – such were the words in which they recognized themselves and their own purest purpose. But imperceptibly new tasks and new questions arose, the aspects of the age were displaced and confused, and just as imperceptibly a point was reached at which Schiller's bold message seemed to miss contact with every concrete situation with which we were faced. We saw wars with their blood-drunkenness, and life being staked and yet not won; and so we learned to value life as a good to be preserved and nursed *above* all others, and the fear of earthly things grew stronger upon us than it has ever been.

That is the state in which we find ourselves today. A state of heaviness, in which spiritual responsibilities mean nothing any longer, and tangible possessions mean everything, possessions which men heap around themselves, entrenching themselves as if in a fortress (which for all that they feel to be insecure) against the threatening attacks of cold unreason. A state of dull captivity, in which, like a horn-call from afar, this poet's voice reaches us.

Has he nothing more to say to Germans? What of human dignity, placed in their hands, which sank and can rise again with them? – Pascal called man a dispossessed king, but a king for all that. Schiller, too, draws our attention to that kingdom. He admonishes us to live our life in its fullness, according to the whole divinely-created pattern. Gold, covered over and now washed clear again by the flux of time – that is what the truth he proclaims is like. Life is not to be won if it is never risked. Man is less than himself if he does not transcend himself. Perhaps men are reluctant to think such thoughts. But they feel them again.

However, irradiation by spiritual forces does not follow any fixed laws such as rule the stars in their courses. No one can say: however much you resist, the poetry of the Classical age, Schiller's poetry, will force its way through to a new position of importance in your life. For this is a realm where force is no longer valid, but is subordinate to man's freedom to choose and to refuse. In the world of the spirit the hour comes, too, but one must perceive and accept it, if one is to receive the gift it brings. A question has been put, the answer to which one may well await with bated breath: a question addressed to the spiritual vitality and self-awareness of the German nation. A nation cannot live merely in the present, nor can an individual. With its memory there fades not only what happened at a certain place, at a certain time; its spiritual form fades too. And it is this alone which makes men citizens and members of the world around them. Germans will either live in the consciousness of what is theirs, or else they will cease to exist as a nation.

SELECT BIBLIOGRAPHY

*

A. COLLECTED WORKS
Several editions are available, the one still most commonly used
as the basis of Schiller studies being the *Säkular Ausgabe*:
Schillers Sämtliche Werke, ed. E. von der Hellen, 16 vols., Stutt-
gart and Berlin 1904–05.
A new complete edition, of which five volumes have so far
appeared, is the Weimar edition:
Schillers Werke. Nationalausgabe.

B. CORRESPONDENCE
Schillers Briefe, ed. F. Jonas, 7 vols., Stuttgart, Leipzig, Berlin,
Vienna, 1892–96.
Briefwechsel zwischen Schiller und Körner, ed. L. Gaiger, 4 vols.,
Stuttgart 1893.
Briefwechsel zwischen Schiller und Wilhelm von Humboldt, ed. A.
Leitzmann, Stuttgart 1900.
Briefwechsel zwischen Schiller und Cotta, ed. W. Vollmer, Stuttgart
1876.
Briefwechsel zwischen Schiller und Goethe, ed. F. Muncker, 4 vols.,
Stuttgart and Berlin 1892.

C. CRITICAL BIOGRAPHIES AND STUDIES
Buchwald, Reinhard: *Schiller*, 2 vols., Leipzig 1937.
Carlyle, Thomas: *The Life of Friedrich Schiller*, 2nd ed.,
London 1845.
Düntzer, Heinrich: The Life of Schiller, trans. Pinkerton,
London 1883.
Garland, H. B.: *Schiller*, London 1949.
Wiese, Benno von: *Friedrich Schiller*, Stuttgart 1959.
Witte, W.: *Schiller*, Oxford 1949.

A SHORT CHRONOLOGY
OF SCHILLER'S LIFE
AND MAIN WORKS

*

1759 November 10. Johann Christoph Friedrich Schiller born at Marbach, Württemberg, second child (and only son) of six. Father (Kaspar Schiller) lieutenant in the service of Duke Karl Eugen of Württemberg (1737–93).

1763 Family settles at Lorch after short period in Schwäbisch-Gmünd. Schiller receives early education and grounding in Latin at village school.

1766 Father stationed at Ludwigsburg. Schiller sent to *Latein-schule* there, with view to education for the ministry. Friendship with Wilhelm von Hoven.

1773 Duke Karl Eugen interferes and places Schiller in his *Karlsschule*.

1775 *Karlsschule* moves to Stuttgart. Schiller and Hoven transferred to newly-created medical faculty. Readings in Klopstock and first poetic attempts.

1779 Goethe visits *Karlsschule* in company of Duke Karl August of Weimar (December 12). Schiller's dissertation rejected: he is told he must remain a further year.

1779–80 Composition of *Die Räuber*.

1780 December 14. Schiller leaves *Karlsschule* to take up post of regimental surgeon in Stuttgart.

1781 Raises loan to pay for publication of *Die Räuber*. Friendship with Andreas Streicher. Relationship with his landlady, Luise Vischer ('Laura'). *Die Räuber* accepted by Dalberg for performance at Mannheim theatre. Visit to Schubart in Asperg fortress.

1782 January 13. First performance of *Die Räuber* at Mannheim. Karl Eugen forbids Schiller further literary activity.

May. Publication of *Anthologie auf das Jahr* 1782. Work on *Fiesko*. Visit to Mannheim in company of Henriette and Lotte von Wolzogen and Luise Vischer. Dalberg promises employment.

September 22. Schiller and Streicher flee to Mannheim.

October. They move to Sachsenhausen to escape detection. Schiller accepts Frau von Wolzogen's offer of refuge at Bauerbach.

December 7. Arrives at Bauerbach. Meeting in Meiningen with W. F. Reinwald.

1783 Work on *Luise Millerin* and *Don Carlos*. Love for Lotte von Wolzogen. Dalberg offers post of *Theaterdichter*.

July. Schiller leaves for Mannheim.

Contract for Dalberg and election to *Deutsche Gesellschaft*. Serious illness in autumn.

1784 January 11. First performance of *Fiesko*.

April 15. First performance of *Kabale und Liebe*. Visit to Frankfurt.

June. Lecture: *Die Schaubühne als eine moralische Anstalt betrachtet*.

Difficulties and disappointments at Mannheim.

Meeting with Frau von Lengefeld and daughters Karoline and Lotte.

Invitation to Leipzig from C. G. Körner and friends.

Marriage of Reinwald and Schiller's sister Christophine.

Relationship with Charlotte von Kalb.

December. Visit to court of Darmstadt. Reads from *Don Carlos* to Duke Karl August of Weimar. Receives title of *Rat* from him.

1785–87 Break with Dalberg.

March 1785. Schiller publishes *Rheinische Thalia*. *Brief eines reisenden Dänen*.

April 1785. Leaves for Leipzig.

Lives with Körner, Huber, Dora and Minna Stock.

Don Carlos completed.

August 27, 1787. First performance of *Don Carlos* in Hamburg.

Works in prose and verse: *An die Freude* (1786), *Der Verbrecher aus verlorener Ehre* (1786), *Der Geisterseher* (1787).

Refuses Schröder's offer of Hamburg post.

Love for Henriette von Arnim.

1787 July. Schiller travels to Weimar. Goethe absent in Italy.

Meetings with Duchess Anna Amalia, Charlotte von Kalb, Wieland, Herder, Charlotte von Stein.

Work on *Geschichte des Abfalls der vereinigten Niederlande*. Meeting with Karl August.

Visit to Jena. Reinhold interests him in Kant's writings.

November. Visit to Bauerbach. Visit (in company of his friend Wilhelm von Wolzogen) to the Lengefelds at Rudolstadt.

1788 Poem: *Die Götter Griechenlands*.

September. First meeting with Goethe.

December. Appointed Professor of History at Jena.

1789 May. Move to Jena and inaugural lecture.

December. Engagement to Charlotte von Lengefeld.

Works: Novelle *Spiel des Schicksals*, poems *Die Künstler* and *Das Glück*.

1790 February 22. Marriage at Wenigen-Jena.

Lectures on history, aesthetics of tragedy.

Writes *Geschichte des dreissigjährigen Krieges*.

1791 January. Severe illness. Nursed by students, among them Novalis. Intensive study of Kant.

December. Danish admirers offer financial assistance.

1792 Summer. Visit to Körners in Dresden.

Autumn. Visit to Jena of Schiller's mother and sister.

1793 August. Departure on visit to Ludwigsburg.

September. Birth of son (Karl Friedrich).

October. Death of Duke Karl Eugen.

Treatise: *Über Anmut und Würde*.

1794 Spring. Publisher Cotta engages Schiller to edit a political journal; this becomes *Die Horen*.

May. Return to Jena.

Friendship with Wilhelm von Humboldt and J. G. Fichte. Gains Goethe's support for *Die Horen*.

July-August. Beginning of close association with Goethe. Writes the *Aesthetische Briefe*.

1795 Schiller declines call to Tübingen university.

Contact with Hölderlin.

Treatise: *Über naïve und sentimentalische Dichtung*.

1796 Death of Schiller's father and sister Nanette.

July. Birth of second son (Ernst).

1796–97 August Wilhelm and Karoline Schlegel in Jena. Meets

frequently Friedrich Schlegel, Jean Paul Richter, Clemens Brentano.

Collaborates with Goethe in the *Xenien*.

Autumn 1786. First appearance of *Musenalmanach*.

Writes numerous poems and ballads ('*Das Balladenjahr*' 1797).

Returns to drama.

1798   Completes first part of *Wallenstein* (begun in 1793).

October 12. First performance of *Wallensteins Lager* at Weimar.

1799   January 30. First performance of *Die Piccolomini* at Weimar.

April 20. First performance of *Wallensteins Tod* at Weimar.

October. Birth of daughter (Caroline).

1800   *Das Lied von der Glocke.*

June 14. First performance of *Maria Stuart* at Weimar.

1801   September 18. First performance of *Die Jungfrau von Orleans* at Leipzig.

Treatise: *Über das Erhabene.*

1802   April. Death of Schiller's mother. Move to Weimar.

November. Schiller raised to nobility by Emperor Francis.

1803   March 19. First performance of *Die Braut von Messina* at Weimar.

1804   March 17. First performance of *Wilhelm Tell* at Weimar. Schiller considers leaving Weimar.

May. Visit to Berlin. Audience with Queen of Prussia. Possibility of Berlin appointment.

May 21. Returns to Weimar. Abandons thought of parting from Goethe.

July. Severe recurrence of illness. Birth of second daughter (Emilie).

Work on *Demetrius* and translations.

November. Writes *Die Huldigung der Künste* for arrival of Grand Duchess Maria Pavlovna.

1805   Fresh outbreak of illness.

April 28. Last meeting with Goethe.

May 9. Schiller dies.

DESCRIPTIVE LIST OF THE
PRINCIPAL PLAYS

*

Die Räuber (The Robbers)

Franz Moor persuades his father to disinherit his brother Karl on
account of his dissolute student life at Leipzig. Karl, on receipt of
this news, is overcome with disgust at the injustice of the world;
when his companions propose to form a band of robbers, he agrees
to become their leader. His sweetheart Amalia rejects Franz and
declares her love for Karl. Count Moor is overcome with grief when
he receives the false news of his son's death. Karl finds himself
increasingly involved in the excesses committed by his band, and
has to swear that he will never desert them. He resolves to visit his
home and Amalia. Returning home in disguise, he learns that
Amalia still loves him and that Franz is responsible for his having
been disowned. He frees his father, who has been incarcerated by
Franz, and determines on revenge. Franz, tormented by fear and his
bad conscience, is in despair. When the castle is stormed by the
robbers, he throttles himself. Count Moor, filled with remorse,
realizes that his son is a robber and murderer, and dies. The robbers
remind Karl of his oath. Amalia compels him to kill her, whereupon
he gives himself up to justice, acknowledging that social justice is
not to be promoted by such methods as his.

Die Verschwörung des Fiesko zu Genua
(The Conspiracy of Fiesco at Genoa)

Fiesko, ambitious for power, has himself made leader of a plot
against the House of Doria, rulers of Genoa, in order to further his
own plans. Old Andreas Doria has deserved well of the Republic,
but his nephew (and heir) Gianettino, a dissolute and violent man,
represents a threat to the liberty of the state. When Gianettino

commits an act of violence against Berta, the daughter of Verrina, the insurrection breaks out. Fiesko is in the Dorias' confidence and thus able to deceive them and introduce soldiers into the town. The coup is successful. In the fighting Gianettino is killed, but Fiesko strikes down a masked figure whom he later discovers to be his own wife. The Dorias flee, and the people make Fiesko their duke. When he rejects Verrina's plea that he should renounce such unrepublican power, the latter thrusts him into the sea from the gangplank of a galley, and he drowns. Andreas Doria returns and restores order.

Kabale und Liebe (Love and Intrigue)

Luise Miller, a musician's daughter, is in love with Ferdinand, the son of President Walter; Miller disapproves, and the President also decides to prevent the unsuitable match by marrying his son off to the Duke's favourite, Lady Milford, who herself desires it. Ferdinand refuses and reproaches her for accepting gifts from the Duke which are purchased with the sufferings of his people. The President threatens violence to Luise's father if the young couple defy him, but Ferdinand averts the danger by threatening to reveal the methods by which his father has risen to power. Wurm, the secretary to the President, who himself desires Luise, persuades the President to let him separate the lovers by arousing Ferdinand's jealousy. Miller is arrested, and Luise is prevailed upon to obtain his release by writing a compromising letter to the Chamberlain, Kalb, which Ferdinand is then allowed to find. He challenges Kalb, who blurts out the truth, but is not believed by Ferdinand. Luise shames Lady Milford, who promises to leave the country. When challenged by Ferdinand, Luise acknowledges the letter, whereupon he poisons them both. Before they die she confesses the truth, and Ferdinand denounces his father.

Don Carlos

Don Carlos is unhappy because he loves his stepmother, who was his own betrothed before his father, King Philipp II of Spain, made her his Queen. His school-friend the Marquis Posa, returned to Madrid after a long absence, hopes to use Carlos to further his own plans for the freedom of the Spanish Netherlands, and arranges a meeting between Carlos and the Queen. She persuades him to renounce his love for her and to devote himself to helping his people. He accordingly asks his father, who despises him, for the command of the army which is leaving for the Netherlands; Philipp refuses and appoints Alba instead. Carlos betrays his love for the Queen to the Princess Eboli, who from jealousy reveals her knowledge to his enemies. The King cannot believe in the Queen's guilt and thinks he has found in Posa a friend he can trust; he instructs Posa to observe them. Posa persuades Carlos to escape and lead the revolt in the Netherlands; in order to gain the King's confidence he obtains permission to arrest Carlos if necessary. Carlos thinks his friend has betrayed him and takes Eboli into his confidence. Posa has Carlos arrested to prevent a fatal disclosure, but is too late; to save him, he confesses that he himself loves the Queen; Philipp has Posa assassinated. His sacrifice was in vain; Carlos' plans to flee are discovered, and he is handed over to the Grand Inquisitor.

Wallenstein

I. *Wallensteins Lager* (*Wallenstein's Camp*). In the Imperial camp at Pilsen it becomes clear to the soldiery that a move is being made to weaken the army, the source of Wallenstein's strength. The nature of his troops' loyalty is shown in the reaction of the various groups to this news and to the attack upon him by the capuchin.

II. *Die Piccolomini* (*The Piccolomini*). It is revealed that Wallenstein's trusted lieutenant, Octavio Piccolomini, has been empowered by the Emperor to render Wallenstein harmless should the latter attempt defection. Octavio's son, Max, loves Wallenstein's daughter, Thekla, and declares unconditional support for her father. Wallenstein is urged by his generals Illo and Terzky to anticipate his dismissal by joining the Swedes, but the astrological signs are unfavourable, and he hesitates. Thekla warns Max against Countess Terzky and resolves to resist her father's ambitious plans for her. The other generals are tricked into signing a declaration of loyalty to Wallenstein, but the trick is discovered. Octavio reveals to his son Wallenstein's traitorous intentions, but Max refuses to believe him. At this point the news arrives of the capture of Wallenstein's negotiator with the Swedes. Max determines to demand the truth from Wallenstein.

III. *Wallensteins Tod* (*The Death of Wallenstein*). Favourable astrological omens indicate that the time for action has arrived. Wallenstein learns of his intermediary's capture; urged by Illo and Countess Terzky to make a pact with the Swedish mediator, Wrangel, he finally agrees. Octavio now sets about ensuring the gradual defection of Wallenstein's troops. Max implores Wallenstein to reconsider and, when he refuses, leaves him. Soon only Terzky's and Buttler's regiments remain loyal to Wallenstein. Wallenstein refuses to consider Max's suit for Thekla; Max parts from her and leads his regiment to their death. Wallenstein orders a move to Eger. Buttler, whom Octavio has turned against Wallenstein, plots the latter's murder with his few remaining supporters. Wallenstein refuses to believe his astrologer's warnings about danger from false friends, and is murdered. Octavio has lost everything, and his appointment to the command of the army only adds to his distress.

Maria Stuart

Mary, a prisoner at Fotheringay, learns through Mortimer that she is to be condemned to death for her part in the Babington plot. She is innocent of the charge but conscious of her guilty complicity in her husband's murder years before. Mortimer assures her of his loyalty and persuades her to approach Leicester in the hope of obtaining a meeting with Queen Elizabeth. She receives Burleigh's announcement of the death sentence with proud composure. The Queen seems to have determined on Mary's death, but Shrewsbury's and Leicester's intervention and Mary's petition appear to move her towards a meeting; however, she engages Mortimer to do away with Mary secretly, a plan with which he ostensibly falls in. Leicester's flatteries and persuasions prevail, and she consents to a meeting. The meeting is disastrous. Mary pockets her pride and humbles herself to ask for mercy. Elizabeth heaps scorn upon her, whereupon Mary in her turn resorts to invective and thus seals her doom. Mortimer claims Mary as the reward for his loyalty: this is the moment of her deepest humiliation. Leicester saves himself by betraying Mary, Mortimer kills himself when his plot fails. Elizabeth signs the death-warrant and hands it to her secretary without precise instructions. Burleigh takes it in order to carry out the sentence immediately. In the face of death Mary regains her composure and receives absolution and communion from Melvil, who has had himself ordained for that purpose. Leicester is shattered by her death and forgiveness, and Elizabeth, attempting to put the blame upon her minions, finds herself guilty and abandoned.

Die Jungfrau von Orleans (*The Maid of Orleans*)

Joan refuses her father's demand that she should take a husband as her sisters have done: she has received a divine command to save her country from the English; success will be hers if she renounces the love of men. The French fortunes are at their lowest ebb; the troops are revolting through lack of pay; the negotiations with Burgundy have broken down, and finally the brave Dunois deserts the feeble King – then news arrives of a victory won through Joan's miraculous intervention. She herself arrives, recognizes the King hiding among his courtiers, and persuades him to give her command of the army. The enemy is dismayed by Joan's success, and Queen Isabeau has difficulty in keeping the peace between the English commanders and the Duke of Burgundy. After a further victory Joan succeeds in reconciling Burgundy and the King. Dunois and La Hire declare their love for her, but she remains true to her vow. The English leader Talbot is killed in a battle before Rheims; a mysterious Black Knight warns Joan of her coming downfall. She defeats the Englishman Lionel in single combat, but then, touched by love and pity, spares his life. Joan is now conscious of having betrayed her mission; when her father accuses her publicly of witch-craft, her sense of guilt prevents her from defending herself, and she is banished. Wandering in the forest during a storm, Joan is captured by the English and imprisoned in a tower under Lionel's guard. She resists his advances and thus recovers her integrity. The French attack, and the King is captured, whereupon Joan breaks her fetters with supernatural strength, rushes into the battle, rescues the King and dies on the victorious field, her mission accomplished.

Die Braut von Messina (*The Bride of Messina*)

The ruler of Messina had learnt in a dream that the birth of a daughter would bring enmity and ruin to his two sons and the kingdom, whilst his wife had dreamt that she would bring love to them. When a daughter, Beatrice, was born, her mother had her secretly taken to a convent, where she was brought up. The brothers' enmity becomes open conflict after their father's death. Isabella, their mother, at last brings about a reconciliation and tells them that they have a sister, for whom she has already sent. The sons then tell their mother that they will present their betrothed to her: each has, un-known to the other, met and fallen in love with Beatrice, Manuel when he found the convent whilst out hunting, Cesar at their father's funeral. On hearing that she is in the town again, Cesar seeks her out, reveals his identity to her and leaves a guard for her protection. A report that she has been abducted by corsairs sends them hurrying to her rescue; Manuel reaches her first, and Cesar, finding her in Manuel's arms, kills him before explanations can be offered, then hurries off to seek his sister, sending Beatrice to their mother. Their identities are now revealed, and Cesar kills himself in expiation of his crime.

Wilhelm Tell

The first act depicts the growing resentment of the Swiss against the oppressive rule of Austria. Baumgarten is saved by Tell from the minions of the local castellan, whom he has killed in defence of his wife's honour; Werner Stauffacher's wife urges him to take council with his friends; Berta von Bruneck represents the nobility who support their countrymen, Ulrich von Rudenz, her suitor, favours accommodation with the foreign rulers; Arnold von Melchtal hears of his father's cruel blinding, and persuades Walter Fürst and Stauffacher to call a secret council on the Rütli. The representatives of Uri, Schwyz and Unterwalden resolve on the Rütli that force is the only way out, and decide that the fortresses shall be stormed at Christmas. Tell, who has refused to take part in these deliberations, is arrested with his son Walter at Altdorf for failing to salute the Hat of Austria. Rudenz, who has been converted to patriotism by his love for Berta, intercedes for him with the Viceroy, Gessler. The latter promises Tell his life if he can shoot an apple from his son's head. He does this, but when, in answer to Gessler's question, he replies that the second arrow he stuck in his belt was for Gessler if the first shot had hit his son, Gessler has him arrested. Tell escapes from the boat conveying him to Küssnacht. Rudenz is now accepted as the people's leader, and plans immediate action to rescue Tell. Tell waylays Gessler on the road to Küssnacht and shoots him down. The revolt breaks out and is overwhelmingly successful. Rudenz rescues Berta from the castle in which she has been imprisoned. It is learnt that the Emperor has been murdered. On the way home Tell meets a monk who reveals himself as the Emperor's murderer, and rejects him with horror. The people acclaim Tell as their saviour, and Berta gives her hand to Rudenz, who frees all his serfs.

INDEX

*